D0252209

Best Answers to the 201 Most Frequently Asked Questions about Getting into College

Mary Kay Shanley

Julia Johnston

McGraw-Hill

New York   Chicago   San Francisco   Lisbon   London   Madrid
Mexico City   Milan   New Delhi   San Juan   Seoul
Singapore   Sydney   Toronto

The McGraw·Hill Companies

Copyright © 2005 by Mary Kay Shanley and Julia Johnston. All rights reserved. Printed in the United States of America. Except as permitted under the United States Copyright Act of 1976, no part of this publication may be reproduced or distributed in any form or by any means, or stored in a database or retrieval system, without the prior written permission of the publisher.

1 2 3 4 5 6 7 8 9 0 AGM/AGM 0 9 8 7 6 5 4

ISBN 0-07-143211-6

McGraw-Hill books are available at special quantity discounts to use as premiums and sales promotions, or for use in corporate training programs. For more information, please write to the Director of Special Sales, McGraw-Hill Professional, Two Penn Plaza, New York, NY 10121-2298. Or contact your local bookstore.

 This book is printed on recycled, acid-free paper containing a minimum of 50% recycled, de-inked fiber.

Library of Congress Cataloging-in-Publication Data

Shanley, Mary Kay.
  Best answers to the 201 most frequently asked questions about getting into college / by Mary Kay Shanley and Julia Johnston.
      p. cm.
  Includes index.
  ISBN 0-07-143211-6 (alk. paper)
1. College student orientation—United States. 2. Universities and colleges—United States—Admission. 3. Study skills. 4. College choice. I. Title: Best answers to the two-hundred one most frequently asked questions about getting into college. II. Johnston, Julia. III. Title.
  LB2343.32.S516   2004
  378.1'61—dc22

                                                                            2004012001

Contents

Acknowledgments

While researching and writing this book, we asked many more than 201 questions. We are grateful to all who have shared their expertise, time, and stories about the college search and application process. We also thank all those others who've helped us with this exercise both personally and professionally through the years.

In addition to those named in the book, we'd like to thank our agent, Grace Freedson; teachers Laurie Amsler and Jim Tredway, Roosevelt High School, Des Moines, Iowa; teacher Rickie Pashler, Lincoln High School, Des Moines; teacher Karen Downing, Valley High School, West Des Moines; Nancy Ankeny, Outreach Representative, College Planning Center, Des Moines; Heather Berg, Editor, American Association of State Colleges and Universities, Washington, D.C.; Alan Beste, Administrative Assistant, Iowa High School Athletic Association, Boone; Alice M. Book, Family Education Coordinator, Alliance for the Mentally Ill of Iowa, Urbandale; Kristin Carnahan, Associate Director of Public Affairs, the College Board, New York, New York; Patricia Farrant, Assistant Vice President, ACT, Iowa City; Mary Gibb, counselor, Valley High School, West Des Moines; George Miller, Director, Network and Technical Services, Drake University, Des Moines; Barmack Nassirian, Associate Executive Director, the American Association of Collegiate Registrars and Admissions Officers, Washington, D.C.; Tony Pals, Director of Public Information, the National Association of Independent Colleges and Universities, Washington, D.C.; Dr. Phyllis Staplin, Director of Curriculum, West Des Moines Community Schools; Jim Sumner, Dean of Admission and Financial Aid, Grinnell College, Grinnell, Iowa; Consumer Credit Counseling Service of Nebraska, Lincoln; and the College Planning Center, a division of Iowa Student Loan Liquidity Corporation, West Des Moines.

Finally, we appreciate our children—Shanley, Jason, and Amy Rhodes; and Jim, John, and McCrystie Adams—for causing us to embark on the search and application quest to make sure they did leave the nest for the colleges that were the best match for them. And a very special thanks to our husbands, Dennis Rhodes and James Adams, who interrupted their day jobs many times for advice, secretarial chores, and unstinting good humor when deadlines loomed.

Mary Kay Shanley
Julia Johnston

Introduction:
Why Do You Need
This Book?

Best Answers to the 201 Most Frequently Asked Questions about Getting into College promises you just that. At first glance, this might seem a ridiculous number of questions to ask about any topic. But consider two things: First, this book doesn't aim to get you into just any college, but rather, into a college that is a good fit for you and the institution. After all, pairing with a particular college is one of the most important decisions you'll ever make. Second, to get from high school to college, you'll have to twist and turn through more than one maze. Quite frankly, it will be a puzzle like you've never experienced.

With all that in mind, 201 questions sounds sensible, right?

We wrote this Q&A book for high school students like you and your parents or guardians. True, it's the student who, sooner or later, will be heading off to college. But the decisions that must be made to get to campus are so big, and the price tag so high, that the whole process becomes a family affair. The decisions vary a bit for each child in a family, except for the price tag thing, which seems to just get higher. As a result, we answer a lot of questions about costs and scholarships.

We know the good, bad, and ugly of the college search and application game because we've been down the road you're just starting—six times, actually. With a lot of help from our husbands, we each raised three children, all of whom earned college degrees. They went one by one, starting the search at different times during their high school careers, looking at a variety of colleges throughout the country. There were questions, dilemmas, research issues, dead ends, Eureka moments, tense conversations, agonizing hours (and days, and—sometimes—weeks), essay rewrites, challenging on-campus interviews, tough decisions to make, and in the end, good decisions made. Going through that with each of our children gave us plenty of experience. By the time the youngest of the six was off packing, we'd learned so much that, as professional writers, we decided that sharing the information would be a good idea.

But the answers flow from more than just our personal experience. In the course of our ongoing research, we have spoken with more than 100 parents whose children have gone to college, as well as with college admissions and financial aid representatives, private college guidance counselors, high school teachers and guidance counselors, and high school students looking for the right college.

Best Answers to the 201 Most Frequently Asked Questions about Getting into College addresses the questions prospective college students and their parents need answers to:

❑ Should I work while I'm in high school since I need the money? Or should I take harder classes and spend more time studying so my grades will be better?

❑ How will I pay for college? Will I have a huge debt when I graduate?

❑ Will high school noncore classes carry any weight on my transcript?

❑ How can I best prepare for the SAT/ACT tests?

❑ As I begin the college search process, do I have information on community, state, private, and highly selective colleges?

❑ Do I have a major in mind? If yes, what draws me to that field?

❑ Is touring the colleges that interest me important? How will I know what to look for?

❑ Are freshmen at the colleges I like guaranteed dorm space?

❑ Should I go Greek?

❑ What if I get homesick?

We've also included four other highlighted, quick-reading features: *Ask yourself, Memo, My experience,* and *Internet savvy.* Combined with all those Q&As, these features will provide a solid basis for your decision making. Each of these features will be pointed out by an accompanying icon, as depicted:

 Ask yourself

 Memo

My experience

 Internet savvy

Ask yourself offers thoughtful questions that can't be answered with a simple yes or no. Instead, they require you to consider your feelings, likes, dislikes, personal values, and how all that stacks up against the reality of your everyday life, colleges you consider, and, ultimately, the college you choose.

> If you are a very, very busy high school student, might you be on activity overload? Were the choices that got you to this point well thought out? Will all your activities hamper your grades? Your health? Would you be better off saying no to some of your current commitments?

> What types of colleges appeal to you? A big or small college? One close to home or far away? A school in the middle of a big city or one that's the central focus of town? Where will you thrive best?

Memo mimics a note you might stick on a bulletin board or refrigerator. For example, some Memos are simple lists:

❑ Five best reasons to take a high school class
❑ Five worst reasons to take a high school class
❑ Eight ways to save dollars
❑ Financial aid key terms

Other Memos are fill-in-the-blank or checklists.

Rate each school you visit: the condition of its dorms, the people with whom you spoke, the distance from school to home, and other qualifiers.

To make sure your college application essay is mistake-proof, check off tips such as using complete sentences, starting every paragraph with a topic sentence, staying within the word limit, and having another person proofread your essay.

In *My experience*, more than 50 students tell how they handled particular situations. Who better to share experiences with you than students who have just gone through the college search process? You can't get more firsthand than that.

Maya Pratt of the University of Chicago successfully balanced academics with sports when she was a high school student.

Timothy Crear chose to enroll at Tougaloo (Mississippi) College, a historically black school.

Boris Shcharansky wrote a convincing I-still-want-to-come letter after learning he was deferred at the University of Pennsylvania in Philadelphia. He was later accepted.

Chrisy Muhler roomed with her high school friend at Ball State University in Muncie, Indiana, and it didn't work at all.

Internet savvy guides you in using the computer to make your college search and applications faster. Because computers are ubiquitous in schools, libraries, cafés, and homes, we assume you have a basic operating knowledge for how to get on the Internet and do a Google or a Yahoo! search. Also, we generally don't provide Web site addresses because they change too quickly.

Topics include the search, entrance requirements, calculating costs, SAT/ACT test dates and sites, applying, and essay writing.

As you imagine your college life, spend some time with this handy book. The Contents is your chronological guide for what you do to get into college, and when you do it. And if you want to skip around, the Contents will help you find what you want quickly. Enjoy the challenging puzzle you're solving for your college future, and thanks for taking this book along with you.

Part 1
Start Here

1

Who You Need to Know— and What You Need to Do

Between right now and the day you've lived the last chapter of this book, a ton of changes are going to occur in your world. True, you'll be older, but the big difference is you'll be a whole lot wiser about what it takes to succeed in the college search and prep process. You'll understand the who, what, when, where, why, and how of that process, and you'll be paired with a college that's just right for you.

Your journey toward college will be complicated, time-consuming, challenging, unclear, and even fun. But you won't have to travel that journey alone. There are plenty of people anxious to help. In fact, identifying those people should be the first step in your journey.

Counselors and Teachers: What They Can Do for You

From the get-go, your high school guidance counselor and certain teachers will play a prominent role in your college search and prep process. After all, your counselor's job is to assist you in navigating the high school maze so you come out on the college doorstep. Good counselors help find answers to such strategic questions as: How much high school math do I have to take? How do I begin figuring out which colleges to even think about? What about entrance exams? When is the next college fair? How is my family ever going to pay for all this education? Additionally, some colleges may ask for a letter of recommendation from your counselor, so establishing a good working relationship with him or her makes sense.

All your teachers have the same job—to help you succeed in school. But some will also play a role in your college search. They become your advocates, sounding boards, and support system. You'll come to depend upon them for academic assistance, friendly advice, and maybe even a letter of recommendation later on.

Identifying Key People

Aside from your parents, counselor, and some teachers, other key people will emerge. You might find support from a school or recreational league coach, an extracurricular activity advisor, your principal, a relative, family friend, mentor, employer, or perhaps someone affiliated with your place of worship.

These people won't show up with "I'm here to help" tattooed on their foreheads, though. Rather, the relationship will evolve as you show respect, interest, and commitment to whatever you are doing and the key person takes a special interest in you. Then you'll find yourself turning to that person in search of advice.

Naturally, not everyone who offers help or advice will necessarily have the same agenda or understand where you are coming from. Peter Brown

Six Surefire Ways to Turn Key People into Advocates

1. Take your college search seriously. When others realize your attitude and sense your maturity, they'll be anxious to help.

2. Don't wait for or expect these key people to do for you what you can do yourself.

3. If you need one-on-one time to discuss specific issues, ask when the key person is available. Then be punctual, whether the discussion is over the phone or in person.

4. Write down all your questions or issues ahead of time.

5. Be a good listener, but if you don't understand something, say so. This process you're involved in is not simple, and there are no dumb questions.

6. If you disagree with advice, speak up. Expressing yourself in a respectful manner may move both of you forward and result in a better decision for you.

Who's on My List of Favorites?

❑ Which teachers seem particularly supportive of me, both inside the classroom and out?

❑ What's my relationship with the counselor to whom I've been assigned? Is he or she helpful? Does the counselor seem interested in me, or do I have to introduce myself every time we talk? (If you have concerns, share them with your parents.)

❑ Are there certain coaches and/or advisors with whom I feel more comfortable?

❑ Which adults outside of school and my family are important to me?

recalls talking to his principal after being admitted to Harvard: "The principal made kind of a haphazard list of good schools and said, 'You know, Peter, the University of Chicago and Rice and even some departments at the University of Oklahoma are really good.'" Ultimately, you weigh information from all possible sources and decide what's best for you.

Your Grade Point Average Counts—Starting in Ninth Grade

Bottom line on your GPA is that it counts *for all four years* of high school. You can put off paying attention to it until you're a senior, but the GPA that will be mailed to prospective colleges will still reflect the average of all of your classes throughout your entire high school career—not just the stellar grades you pull off as a senior.

Why is that little number so important? Because college admissions officers say GPA is one of the biggest indicators of how well you will do in college academically. (The other indicator is the level of difficulty in the high school courses you take.) The higher your GPA, the more colleges you should be able to consider. A good GPA and class rank (which compares your GPA to other members of your class) may also impact scholarship and grant money from the college or other sources.

Your Path to a Good GPA

- ❏ Pay attention to grades from day one of freshman year.
- ❏ If you're having difficulty with a particular subject, ask to meet with the teacher. Ignoring the problem makes it get worse, not disappear.
- ❏ If you're having a problem getting along with or learning from a particular teacher, the best solution is to talk with the teacher. However, this may be easier said than done. The next best thing may be to talk with your counselor and parents about how to approach the issue.
- ❏ Understand what you can do for extra credit to boost your grade.
- ❏ Midterm grades indicate problems that you still have time to rectify.

Class Selection

Some states require that every high schooler take a specific number of courses in core subjects to graduate. Other states offer guidelines only, and the individual districts set requirements. Besides required courses, you'll need to deal with course sequence—taking the prerequisites before you can get into Honors or AP (Advanced Placement) classes. There may be scheduling conflicts, such as when the course you want to take in the second semester is only offered in the first semester. Plus, don't forget about physical education, and electives like business education, band, and driver education. You will need to check the admissions requirements for each college in which you're interested, preferably before your senior year.

It's a complicated process, and making a mistake can impact graduation or college admission. So work with your counselor on class selection. However, because your counselor is helping plenty of other students as well, take advantage of his or her group presentations and handouts, and use any one-on-one counselor time wisely.

Playing It Safe versus Taking Risks

Playing it safe means taking courses you know will result in top grades. Taking risks means signing up for courses where you'll be challenged, learn, and grow, but maybe not get a top grade. Today's college admissions reps prefer that you consider the riskier route—challenge yourself and get a B instead of going for the easy A. That's why admissions reps give extra weight to Honors and AP classes. They see those courses as good predictors of whether you'll succeed academically in college.

As a matter of fact, if you score high enough on an AP test in high school, the college you go to may give you credit for the equivalent college course and/or bump you to a higher-level class. The downside of taking AP exams is that no matter how well you score, some colleges won't accept high school AP coursework in place of their courses. In addition, if you get a C or lower in an AP or Honors class, or if you drop the class to improve your GPA, you may hurt your chances for consideration by a selective school.

The only way to know for sure about AP credits and grades is to ask each college representative, who may refer you to the specific department within the college.

Noncore Classes Count Too

Sometimes, learning just for the fun of it gets lost in the shuffle of required classes. What a shame! Elective courses can introduce you to whole new subject areas (like marine biology), potential careers (like journalism), or artistic skills (like pottery). As with AP and Honors courses, admissions reps like to see a smattering of electives because they indicate a well-rounded student with natural curiosity. Still, if you have to pick between taking trigonometry and peer helpers . . .

Am I an Explorer?

❏ Do I gravitate toward a challenge or shy away?

❏ Have I ever thought about being daring in course selection? For example, if I can't say a word in Russian, would I consider signing up for Russian I?

❏ How do I feel about taking AP classes, knowing they are true college-level courses?

❏ Do I get down or angry if I don't get an A?

❏ Can I handle classmates who don't share my enthusiasm for learning?

❏ Can I see a connection between course selection today and an exciting career down the road?

Nine Keys to Good Study Skills That Really Do Work!

1. Learning to manage your time is just like mastering calculus or a sport. To be successful requires practice, effort, and patience.

2. Keep a notebook for each class and make notes every day regarding what you have to do. Write down assignments and due dates. Oh, and look at it after school each day.

3. Keep a file for each class's handouts and assignments.

4. Have a quiet, well-lit study space that's away from the rest of the family. Study there at the same time—or as close to it as you can come—every day.

5. Allow enough time to study each subject.

6. Study difficult subjects first.

7. Plan ahead for big projects. Remind yourself that if a paper is due the first of December, starting it during Thanksgiving break is not a good idea.

8. If you get hungry or sleepy while studying, take a five- or ten-minute break.

9. Studying a little each day for a test is better than cramming. (You probably knew that.)

Signing Up for the Best Teachers

In the business world, most professionals are paid according to their worth. But in the high school world, teachers almost always are paid on the basis of how long they've been teaching and how much education they've taken beyond their bachelor's degree. It may sound as if the only differences between one teacher and another are seniority and postgraduate classes. But you and your fellow students know there are other differences. Students can always tell you which teachers are hard, easy, interesting, boring, really great, and really not great.

You'll be assigned to teachers you like and ones you don't like. In fact, throughout your whole life, you'll work with people you like and don't like. So you might as well start figuring out how to handle that now. That said, there may be cause for an exception once in a while. For instance, if you just love English and have your heart set on taking composition from a particular teacher, consider a written request for that instructor, including your reasons. Or if you learn best by doing, and a particular history teacher has a reputation for teaching through projects, consider requesting that instructor. If you truly have a personality conflict with a teacher, talk to your counselor about helping you change classes.

NCAA Standards

If you hope to be a student athlete at a Division I or II college, your coach should be talking with you about the eligibility rules by your sophomore year. Still, you may want to visit the NCAA Clearinghouse Web site at www.ncaaclearinghouse.net for a core-course listing for your high school. There's also an NCAA Guide for the College-Bound Student-Athlete and Division I and II initial eligibility requirements.

Five Best Reasons to Take a Class

1. It's in an area you love, one that might even lead to a career.
2. It's challenging and will raise the bar for you as a learner.
3. It will lead to Honors and AP courses.
4. It's a subject about which you've always been curious.
5. It's in an area you don't know anything about.

Five Worst Reasons to Take a Class

1. You'll be with your best friend. Or your boyfriend or girlfriend. Or somebody you wish were your boyfriend or girlfriend.
2. It's a snap; you'll never have to study.
3. Everybody says the teacher's really funny, even though you don't learn a lot.
4. You need three more credits but you don't want to take any 8 a.m. classes, so this one will do.
5. If the class is as tough as they say it is, you can just drop it.

How Do I Learn Best?

One way to select teachers and classes is to think about how you best absorb information.

❏ Do I understand something better when I read it or hear it?

❏ Do I remember what I read better than what I hear?

❏ Do I understand a reading assignment better when I take notes?

❏ Does taking lecture notes help me remember the information better?

❏ Does it help even more to recopy my own lecture notes?

❏ Do I learn better by listening to a lecture than by taking notes from a textbook?

❏ Do I remember points better if I say them out loud?

❏ Do I learn best when I study with other people?

❏ Can I picture what I read?

❏ Can I see words in my mind before I spell them?

❏ Do I like to make models?

❏ Would I rather do an experiment or read about it?

❏ Is it hard for me to sit quietly when studying?

❏ Do I pace around when I'm trying to think through a problem?

Distance Learning: Virtual High Schools and College Classes

Lucky you! You're part of one of the biggest overhauls of the teaching/learning process since the concept of a university became reality in medieval Europe. And that was at least 500 years ago! The newest overhaul is distance learning, which began at the college level but is now a real-time factor from kindergarten through twelfth grade. Christa McAuliffe Academy, for example, is a virtual, accredited, private K-12 school headquartered in Yakima, Washington. Not only can you earn your high school diploma through the academy from wherever you live in the United States, but you also can be part of the Student Congress or go to the prom—which is during graduation week, so there's only one trip to Yakima at the end of senior year.

More common are online classes that enable you to receive high school and/or college credit in one of several ways. Interactive telecourses use live video to broadcast the course to your school and perhaps other sites as well. The instructor is on a video screen; students are in classrooms at desks fitted with microphones so they can talk with the instructor and students at other locations. There are also video courses that may be streamed via the Internet, and Web courses that require an active Internet account and a personal computer. The Web classes are presented on the Internet. Finally, combinations of these are becoming common.

Distance Learning

If you begin with www.google.com, type in distance learning classes for high school students. You'll find offerings from high schools, colleges, and universities and for-profit companies. Don't sign up for anything, though, until you ask your counselor about your school's requirements and procedures to follow. Neither high school nor college credit is automatic, no matter what your final grade.

The Pros of Distance Learning

- ❏ You may be able to graduate early.
- ❏ You can fit more classes into a semester.
- ❏ You can take classes not offered at your school.
- ❏ You'll be able to do coursework when it's convenient.
- ❏ The teacher, other students, and resources are only a click away.
- ❏ You'll be able to interact with people throughout your state, country, or even the world.
- ❏ If you got a poor or failing grade in a class at school, you may retake it to improve your grade. You'll still need to ask your counselor about what grade (or grades) will show up on your transcript, however.

The Cons of Distance Learning

❏ Distance learning tends not to work if you aren't disciplined enough to work independently.

❏ You'll be isolated physically, unless technology and class assignments encourage interaction.

❏ It can take longer for class rapport to build, since you, the teacher, and other students may have little background in common.

❏ If you aren't comfortable with the technology, you may hesitate to participate in class discussion.

❏ The motivation that arises from contact with and competition with others in the classroom isn't present.

Is Distance Learning Right for Me?

❏ How hard do I push myself? Is my normal pace going to get the job done?

❏ How well do I work on my own? Am I good at figuring out directions on my own?

❏ Do I have a high degree of comfort with and knowledge of technology?

❏ How do I feel about not being in the same room with the instructor? About not being in the same room with all the other students? What about being the *only* student?

❏ How helpful is classroom discussion for me?

Taking Distance Learning
College Courses in High School

I've taken distance learning courses through Blue Mountain Community College and Eastern Oregon University. I took my first course on campus the summer I was 14. I was a little intimidated. I was the only one at that site. So far, I've taken computer and Internet classes, psychology, advanced biology, and Pre-AP English. I took a weekend class on peer mentorship. I was already mentoring an autistic boy—my neighbor—through the mental health clinic. I found a similar program through BMCC so we got all the materials from the program and I got credit. I've never had a computer malfunction or any difficulty communicating with my teachers or class members.

I earn dual credits for most of my classes. That means I get high school and college credit. The high school teacher has to have the credentials to teach at the college level, and the courses have to match what the college teaches. The high school teacher is my actual instructor and the one who signs off that you can do the tasks. Since my high school didn't offer most of my distance learning classes, my high school advisor also had to sign forms so I could get credit.

I pay $10 per credit hour per class and automatically get college credit if I have a B or better. I've never taken an online test, although more EOU classes are offering that now. Most of my work was graded on papers, assignments, and projects.

When I enter college, I'll have between 57 and 60 credits and so will be halfway through my sophomore year. I think the cost is probably one-tenth of taking the courses in college, and the credits will transfer to the schools I'm looking at. I hope it shows the initiative I want people to see when I apply for jobs and scholarships.

Distance learning classes aren't easy, but if you think you have a chance of succeeding, do it.

Will Burton, Baker High School, Baker City, Oregon

College Entrance Requirements

Generally speaking, most colleges expect you to have:

❏ Two to four years of a foreign language

❏ Four years of English, which can include advanced composition, speech, journalism, and media literacy

❏ Three to four years of math, which can include algebra, geometry, trigonometry, calculus, advanced algebra, analysis, and statistics

❏ Three to four years of science, which can include biology, earth science, chemistry, and physics, including lab work

❏ Three to four years of social studies, which can include geography, U.S. history, U.S. government, world history, anthropology, economics, psychology, and sociology

❏ One to three years of electives such as fine arts, performing arts, computer science, computers, or technology

Actual requirements vary from one school to another—even among state universities in the same state! So check the entrance requirements for each college in which you're interested. And remember to work closely with your counselor.

Powerful Peers

You've probably been hearing about the good, the bad, and the ugly aspects of peer pressure forever. About how peer pressure goes hand in hand with being a teenager. How it can motivate someone to aim for the National Debate Tournament or see how many beers will go down in 30 minutes. If peers can influence what you wear, whom you run around with, and whom you date—and they can—certainly peers can influence what classes you take, how hard you work in school, and even what colleges you consider.

By basing class choices, your willingness to work hard—or not—and your college decision on what everyone else is doing, you might do yourself a disservice. It would be a shame, for example, if you gave up a lifelong dream of being a marine biologist just because everybody in your group decided you should all go to State U, which has no marine biology degree.

Class Scheduling Questions for My Counselor

❏ What are the required and recommended courses for college prep? For high school graduation?

❏ How should I plan my schedule so I get everything in?

❏ What elective courses should I consider?

❏ Which AP courses are available?

❏ What requirements must I meet to be considered for the National Honor Society?

❏ Are there classes that might help me start exploring my interests and related careers?

❏ If my colleges need a recommendation from you, how can I help you know me better so that any recommendation you write is more personal?

Hanging with the Going-to-College Crowd

One of the best ways to handle peer pressure—as far as academics is concerned—is to hang around with kids who plan to go to college too. You all understand why class choices should be based on what's best for each person's future. You all realize that studying is part of daily life. And you respect one another's intellect. That doesn't always happen in high school, where sometimes it seems one of the worst things that can be said about a student is that he or she is smart.

Special Interest Camps and Classes

When you were a little kid, camp usually consisted of hiking down a well-worn trail next to your buddy, then rewarding yourself back at the campsite with s'mores. Now, as a high schooler, going to camp is a bit more serious, although you still might get s'mores at the end of the day. Special interest camps are almost certainly residential (sleepaway), last

Eight Tips for Choosing a Camp

1. Is the camp accredited by an overseeing organization or the state in which it's located?

2. Who is the director? How long has that person been there, and what is his or her philosophy? What are the staff's qualifications and occupations?

3. How important is competitiveness to the director, staff members, and campers?

4. If the camp is one you can go to year after year, what percent of campers actually return? If it's low, ask why.

5. Look at the facilities—if not in person, at least through camp literature or a Web site. Check out sleeping arrangements and toilet/shower facilities.

6. Consider the schedule. Is it a back breaker? A snoozer? Is there room for regular old fun? Free time?

7. What about availability of medical staff?

8. Then, of course, there's the cost.

anywhere from a week to six or even eight weeks, and can cost thousands of dollars. Often, the commitment and hard work required from the camper is equal to—or probably greater than—the effort you put into your regular school classes. Because special interest camps take a lot of (most likely) your parents' money as well as your time and effort, think carefully before signing up.

There's good reason why the camps can lead you to eke out so much hard work. Students choose a camp based on something they love. For example, Hampshire College Summer Studies in Mathematics in Amherst, Massachusetts, attracts mathematically talented high school students. Blue-Chip Basketball Camps in Georgetown, Kentucky, keep kids on the court for a week at a time. Summer Music Camps at Florida State University in Tallahassee offer everything from jazz to opera to music theatre. U.S. Space Camp in Huntsville, Alabama, can shoot you off in all sorts of directions later on—from physicist to astronaut.

Summer classes, on the other hand, generally are offered by your high school, community college, or nearby four-year institution. These classes can get you up-to-speed on a difficult subject, introduce you to a topic you

Search and Compare

Search www.google.com or www.yahoo.com for specific summer camps—basketball, drama, writing. There are also sites such as www.kidscamps.com, which lists a bundle of camps—sports, arts, academics/study abroad, self-improvement, special interests, special needs, winter/spring break, community service, family, and leadership programs. Click a topic and you'll be asked your preference for state, country, religion, gender, region, and session length. You can also indicate "No Preference." You'll receive a list of camps that meet your qualifications. If there are no matches, change one or more of your preferences.

wouldn't have time to explore during the regular school year, or take you beyond what your school curriculum offers.

Informal College Visits

You can begin looking at colleges on an informal basis as a freshman and sophomore. If your family takes summer vacations or periodic road trips, include a drive through college campuses along the way. Walk around campus and stop by the student center for something to drink. Why? Because every college is different, and while you may never, ever consider one of these schools when it's time to get serious, brief excursions will begin to give you a sense of what life might be like after high school graduation.

Go to college sports events—from a Saturday afternoon football game to a weekend of field and track events. Attend a concert or play on campus. Enroll in one of the school's summer programs for people your age.

Read, Read, Read

If you're like most teenagers, you loved reading when you were younger. Trips to the library or the bookstore were treats; escaping with a good book was a great way to spend a few weekend hours; and postponing bedtime by five minutes so you could finish the chapter just made sense. Then along came high school and, hey, what happened? Reading anything beyond what's assigned seems to have gone by the wayside.

Four Key Points to Look For on Campuses

1. Buildings should be attractive and well kept, no matter how old. In fact, some of the most beautiful campuses in this country have the oldest buildings.

2. Walkways should be broad, well lit, and bordered by nice landscaping. True, you're not going to pick a school because of its flowerbeds, but a pleasant, homey environment doesn't hurt.

3. The people you meet should be friendly and welcoming. In fact, it may not be surprising if a faculty member stops to introduce him- or herself.

4. The neighborhood surrounding the campus may be old because many American colleges and universities were built more than a century ago, close to the downtown areas. It is not unusual for the neighborhood bordering the campus to be somewhat run-down.

Actually, high school is when you should be reading more, not less. Reading helps you continue building your vocabulary and grammar skills. Reading and writing (they go hand in hand) are key to every subject you're taking—even math. Plus, because of the information explosion brought on by the Internet, it's more important than at any other time in history for people to understand where to find information and to be able to verify its reliability. That requires not only being a good reader, but also a savvy one. Besides, if you are used to devouring books in high school, you'll have a leg up in college. Right now your teachers probably assign one chapter each night, but some of your professors may assign 100 pages per class meeting.

Reading Almost Anything versus Watching TV

Watching television is a passive experience. You slump in a chair or sprawl out on the floor and stare at a screen. Watching the tube doesn't require you to think or imagine. It doesn't help further develop your skills in word recognition, decoding, vocabulary, spelling, or higher-level thinking. The only thing required of you is that you keep your eyes on the screen. Reading, on the other hand, stimulates your brain and causes your

Five Ways to Get More Out of a Book

1. Before you dive into Chapter 1 of a nonfiction book, read the preface, fore-word, chapter titles, and anything about the author. Also, check the top-ics the Library of Congress deemed important regarding the book, which are on the copyright page in newer books. Similar material is available in fiction books from the Library of Congress or Sears subject headings on the copyright page.

2. With nonfiction, the introduction and chapter summaries the author may have provided should indicate what that author wants you to know. As you read sections in a textbook, pay attention to the size, style, and color of the type. Words in the same style, size, and color indicate the same level of importance. For instance, the chapter title might be all capital let-ters and red; the section titles, large type and blue; the subtitles, purple and smaller. These clues can be used to create an outline or a web of notes.

3. If you are a visual learner, transform a fiction book into a movie in your head to better understand what's going on. If the book has already been made into a movie, see that first. Then, as you read, you can add onto the mental pictures already there.

4. In fiction books, italics or other typeface changes indicate a flashback or shift in time or point of view. Another change, not as common, is when double spacing replaces regular spacing to indicate a shift in place.

5. If reading is somewhat challenging, learn to read between the lines. For ex-ample, you can tell how old a person is by a description of his or her re-sponsibilities (the editor of a school paper is likely to be a senior and 17 or 18), the person's language (a character who says, "Land o' Goshen," is prob-ably grandmotherly), and by actions (the driver of the car could barely reach the gas pedal means he or she is probably less than 16).

creative juices to kick in. You think, interact, and keep on developing the skills that make you a good reader, a good writer, an articulate speaker, and a keen thinker.

Reading *People* versus *Crime and Punishment*

If all those commendations about the benefits of "reading almost anything" are true—and research indicates that is so—then reading quality literature

Finding the Best Book Lists for College Preparation

Go to the American Library Association at www.ala.org. Click "Our Association" on the banner across the top of your screen. Click "Divisions" on the left side of the screen. Click "YALSA" (Young Adult Library Services Association) on the left side of the screen. Click "Booklists & Book Awards" on the left side of the screen. Click "Outstanding Books for the College Bound." In shorthand, click through this series: Our Association/Divisions/YALSA/Booklists & Book Awards/Outstanding Books for the College Bound.

Also, go to the International Reading Association at www.reading.org. Click "Choices Booklists/Young Adults' Choices."

most likely only enhances the benefits. You are exposed to a higher level of vocabulary, a wealth of information you may otherwise bypass, and complex material that hones critical thinking skills. Being a good reader is one of the best heads-up you can give yourself in the college prep process.

End-of-Chapter Questions

1.1 Besides parents, who can help me with my college search and applications? How much input should other people have in my decisions?

1.2 How can teachers help me? Do I have to earn an A in their class for them to want to help me?

1.3 Which people outside of school might help me? How?

1.4 Do I have to ask people to help or will they just do it? How well do they have to know me to help me?

1.5 If I'm friendly with a teacher, does that mean I'm brown-nosing? Will the teacher think I'm just sucking up to get a good recommendation or grade?

1.6 What factors should influence the classes I take?

1.7 What classes do colleges expect to find on my transcript? Are admissions requirements the same for every college?

1.8 Why should I consider taking some elective classes? Do colleges think you are goofing off if you take electives?

1.9 What is an AP class? An Honors class? What do such classes mean in terms of college preparation? How do colleges regard such classes for admission purposes?

1.10 How do I know if a college will give me class credit for my high school AP classes?

1.11 What is distance learning? What are the advantages? Disadvantages? Will it work for me?

1.12 If I take just the classes required in my high school for graduation, will I meet admissions requirements at a variety of colleges?

1.13 What are special interest camps? Are they important in college admissions decisions? Should I go just to pad my résumé for my college application?

1.14 How do I figure out if the camp will meet my needs?

1.15 Why should I visit college campuses before my senior year? What should I look for during informal visits?

1.16 What are the advantages of reading more in high school? Do I have to read only books on "good for me" lists?

2

Extracurricular Activities, Sports, and Community Service

What you do after school, on the weekends, and during your summer months as far as extracurricular activities, sports, and volunteering are concerned, counts. In fact, your choices may tip the scales with college admissions officers down the road. That's especially true at private and highly selective schools, where the admissions reps can be pickier in their search for well-rounded students and class mix.

The College Board, creator of the SAT, says participation in athletics and activities is a better indicator of overall college performance than other yardsticks. And ACT, Inc., creator of the ACT Assessment, says achievement in high school activities is a better predictor of success beyond college than high school or college grades or even high ACT scores. Very few educators would find those statements surprising. That's because getting involved in your school and community beyond the classroom is a great way to learn skills you'll use throughout your life: how to make new friends, realize your talents, and introduce yourself to new experiences. The activities may even steer you toward a career path.

Quality versus Quantity

Counselors see two problems with high school students' involvement in community service and school activities beyond the classroom. One problem is students who don't get involved in anything. During his 30 years as a high school guidance counselor, Jay Cookman of West Des Moines,

Am I on Overload?

- ❏ Do I get as much sleep as I need most nights?
- ❏ Do I have time for at least two balanced meals a day or am I always running out the door with a bag of chips in my hand?
- ❏ Am I getting sufficient exercise?
- ❏ Do I complete house chores as expected, feed the dog, and play with my little brother/sister?
- ❏ Do I enjoy the things I'm involved in or are most of them just one more thing on a full plate? What do I look forward to?
- ❏ Are my goals for what I want out of my commitments realistic?
- ❏ Am I in certain activities because that's what my parents or friends wanted me to join?
- ❏ Am I afraid to back out of something, even if I don't put anything into or get anything out of it?
- ❏ Am I consistently having problems with my friends? Or with my boyfriend or girlfriend?
- ❏ Do I ever have free time where I can do nothing at all?

Iowa, told incoming freshmen (and their parents), "Get involved in something. I don't care whether it's sports or a foreign language club or announcing on the school radio station. You can't only identify with your school through academics. The kids who go to classes then leave right after the last bell rings, usually find other things to do that aren't always good. They're often the ones who end up in trouble. School becomes a bore, and in extreme cases, they drop out."

If not getting involved in anything is one problem, getting involved in everything is the other. Some students have never met a sign-up sheet they didn't like. True, you get quantity out of joining this and that. But because there are only 24 hours in your day, you may not get quality. Belonging to an organization is one thing; going to the meetings, participating in the events, or taking on a leadership position is quite another. Usually, you'll derive few benefits from in-name-only affiliation.

What Colleges Expect of You

College reps are looking for depth. Did you write a couple of articles for the school newspaper, or were you an editor? Did you spend one afternoon painting the backdrop for the school play, or did you design the whole set? Did you work at a homeless shelter one Saturday, or did you mobilize a group who volunteered there for a semester?

Admissions reps consider what you've done in high school as a sign of what you will accomplish in college. They also view college as a two-way street: the institution gives you an education, and your efforts while a student there enhance the institution.

Extracurricular Activities

The reason high schools offer extracurricular activities is because educators like to turn out well-rounded graduates. Students like you participate in activities or join clubs because they're fun or interesting or, better yet, both. The experience helps build character, plus you may walk away with new friends. Extracurricular activities also broaden your focus and slice off some of the stress that comes with studying.

Realize, though, that some classes you take for credit are like extracurricular activities because you spend so much time outside class. For example, marching band may garner you one academic credit toward graduation, but that teensy credit does not really represent the 6 a.m. practices before school even starts in the fall, performances at parades, football games, and competitions, and your practice time for private music lessons. If band takes all your extra time, do not feel compelled to add

How Activities Make Me Stand Out

❏ Employers like well-rounded employees—even high school part-timers—who get along with others. Club memberships help you develop the social skills to accomplish that trait.

❏ Excelling at a particular activity can garner attention within the community beyond school. Just ask someone who had the lead in the school play or performed with the local symphony orchestra.

❏ A college letter of recommendation from your activity's sponsor trumpets the "you" outside of the classroom.

❏ Some scholarship opportunities are available only for students who pursue a specific interest, usually through a club or activity.

Seven Steps to Choosing Activities

1. Set three goals for the school year—goals you can meet by participating in extracurricular activities.

2. Create a list of extracurricular activities that sound interesting; include ones that play on your strengths and ones that would help you correct your weaknesses.

3. Match each extracurricular activity listed with the goal (or goals) that activity would help you achieve.

4. Prioritize your activity-goal list.

5. Now consider other commitments you already have: family, academics, sports, volunteering, or a part-time job.

6. Decide how many of the activities at the top of that prioritized list you can *reasonably* join. If you can't decide what's reasonable, talk to a parent, activity sponsor, or your counselor, because you don't want to overcommit.

7. Go sign up.

other activities to pad your résumé. Instead, consider how you can show on your application your commitment and its effect on your life or decisions about college.

Sports

There are plenty of good (and realistic) reasons to pursue sports in high school; wanting to be a college or professional athlete someday probably shouldn't be one of them. Consider that only 5.6 percent of high school football players go on to play at NCAA member colleges and universities. And only 2 percent of those college players ever play professionally. Likewise, only 3.1 percent of girls who play high school basketball go on to play at NCAA member colleges, and only 1 percent of those college players become professional players.

If you play a high school sport, you're more likely than nonsports participants to eat more healthfully and less likely to smoke cigarettes, drink alcohol, use illicit drugs, engage in sexual activity, and engage in violent activities. Your grades will be higher, your attendance better; you'll be

Time Management Tips

❑ Create a "to do" list each night before bedtime. Block out realistic amounts of time for homework, academic projects, club meetings, and commitments to extracurricular projects. Put the list with your daily planner, calendar, or school schedule.

❑ Be flexible. You'll have interruptions in your schedule every single day.

❑ If you're a perfectionist, try really hard to modify some aspects while still aiming to do the best you can. Striving for perfection usually means paying attention to unnecessary details.

❑ Sometimes, a big project on your list is easier to put off than to take on. But no matter how hard you try, it won't go away. Break the project into smaller parts and tackle them individually. (It works!)

❑ If you implement these suggestions and you're still harried, you may have bitten off more than you can chew. Consider dropping the least interesting activity that causes you the most stress. Dropping out of an activity may be better than participating halfheartedly.

❑ Remember that managing time effectively takes practice and effort.

more likely to attend college and less likely to drop out of high school than nonathletes. Those are some compelling reasons to go run around a track, throw a ball, hit a ball, or jump in the pool.

Coach Has Responsibilities Too

Coach should, first of all, be an educator, just like your classroom teachers. Your school's athletic programs—as well as its extracurricular offerings—are designed to enhance academic achievement and should never interfere with opportunities for academic success.

So what should Coach be teaching? Not only the competitive aspects of your sport, but also the play aspects. After all, one reason high schoolers go out for sports is because it's fun. Additionally, if you hope to play sports at a Division I or II college, beginning sophomore year Coach should talk with you about the NCAA Initial Eligibility Clearinghouse Registration requirements. (Requirements for Division III differ because eligibility for financial aid, practice, and competition is governed by insti-

Getting Overextended with Activities in High School

There were 45 students in my high school graduating class. If your class is small, and not a lot of people like to be involved, then someone like me, who likes to be involved, says, "I'll do it. I'll do it." Pretty soon you're in charge of everything. I'm a natural leader and take charge, even if I'm not supposed to be in charge. I think in high school, there's pressure to be involved because of college applications and scholarships.

I was an officer in FCA, National Honor Society, Spanish Honor Society, cheerleading captain, on student council, played basketball until senior year. At first, it wasn't that bad, but the more involved you get, the more demanding [it is].

High school was pretty much a breeze for me academically. But academics don't come naturally in college; you have to put in effort. If you make the commitments in college you did in high school, you're bogged down. I started signing up, still as involved as ever. Finally, I said, "Phyllis, you know you can't do that so tell them no so they can find somebody else." But I still have a hard time telling people no.

You need to prioritize. Time management is key. I write down everything on a calendar. I have an overview of the month and every day. It sounds like my whole life is planned, but it has to be to get everything done.

Now there's pressure to be involved because I'm going on to a four-year college. People say, "You can use this on your résumé. You can use this on your application." You feel pressured to put your activities on that piece of paper, but there's more to life than that. There's more than being able to say, "I was a member of 15 clubs and got my picture in the yearbook."

Phyllis Scott, Meridian (Mississippi) Community College

tutional, conference, and other NCAA regulations.) And realize that even if you take enough NCAA approved core courses in high school, get an 18 on the ACT or an 820 on the SAT, you still have to meet the admission requirements of each NCAA member school to which you apply.

Good coaches also should make judgments based on what's best for everyone on the team, offer sincere praise, positive reinforcement, and constructive criticism, and mete out discipline without humiliation or embarrassment. Finally, Coach should provide emotional support and guidance when needed.

How Sports Make Me Stand Out

❏ Sports teach me respect, teamwork, good sportsmanship.

❏ Knowing how to win and lose with dignity transfers to areas beyond athletics.

❏ Being able to work hard and with self-discipline makes me valuable as an employee.

❏ I'm building self-confidence and developing skills to handle competitive situations.

What Are My Responsibilities?

❏ To commit at least as much effort to academics as to sports.

❏ To be a good sport, both in practices and competitions.

❏ To attend every practice and game possible and notify Coach when I can't.

❏ To try to improve my performance from the beginning of the season to the end and from one year to the next.

❏ To listen and learn as best I can.

❏ To treat all coaches, teammates, and the opposing team, coaches, and fans with respect.

❏ To have fun, and to tell Coach and my parents if participation stops being fun.

Sometimes, however, Coach and the player aren't on the same page. A player may feel Coach's expectations are unrealistic. Coach may view the player as unwilling to put forth effort. Then, parents get involved. They see Coach playing favorites; Coach sees parents meddling. What to do? Ideally, the solution emerges out of coach-player communication. If that

How I Balanced Academics with Sports

I played club soccer through high school. We practiced four times a week and the commitment was almost year-round. As we got older, some tournaments would be 2,000 miles away.

Academically, I took full loads that weren't light. I had one study hall each semester. I took three AP courses and was involved in activities too. And I graduated with good grades.

Actually, I think the full load and soccer forced me to have time management, which I probably wouldn't have had otherwise. I used a planner and stayed up late, but what was most helpful was getting homework done before soccer— either practice or a game. You're tired afterward. I'd do homework after school, and if I got restless, I'd practice with the soccer ball awhile, then come back inside to do homework. On road trips, I studied on the way to the game; I knew I wouldn't on the way back.

Having a job during the school year would have been too much. And my parents backed off with household chores when I was really busy.

One big motivator was that I knew I wanted to play in college. When you're a freshman or sophomore in high school, you don't really know that. But if you have a sport, keep with it because it may help in the end. The University of Chicago is a highly competitive school, and I think one reason I got in was because of soccer.

Maya Pratt, University of Chicago, Illinois

doesn't work, the athletic director may have to become involved. Issues can get so contentious that school districts typically have formal procedures intended to lead to a resolution.

Making Choices about Your Hobbies

Some students shove their hobbies aside because they get so busy with studies, extracurricular activities, and sports. Other high school students turn childhood hobbies into passions. The student who used to pick away on the guitar might either slip the instrument into its case and join the basketball team or end up in a garage band. The high schooler who spent half a childhood making sandcastles at the beach might gobble up every cre-

What Do I Go After? What Do I Give Up?

❏ What do I just love to do?
❏ What do I have time to do?
❏ What high school options sound appealing?
❏ If I add something new, do I give up something old?

ative art class the school offers or abandon that sculpting talent and go work on the yearbook.

It all comes down to making choices, which is generally hard to do—and even harder when parents, teachers, coaches, or sponsors have vocal opinions. They may have your best interests in mind—or they may want you to pursue something they didn't have the opportunity to go after. A gentle reminder that it's your life is sometimes in order.

Would Community Service Suit Me?

❏ Is the idea of giving something back to my community appealing?
❏ Will volunteering get me to think about others more than I usually do?
❏ How will community service help me learn to be a good citizen?
❏ What kind of community service will teach me about situations and people I wouldn't experience otherwise?
❏ What skills do I need to be a successful volunteer? What skills will I learn?
❏ Should I seek a volunteer position where I can use my skills, learn new skills—or maybe both?
❏ Can I tell from talking with someone in a particular organization whether I'll fit there? What if I sign on for a project and then don't feel comfortable with the project as it unfolds?
❏ If I sign up to work with children, but end up filing papers, should I say something?
❏ Do I understand the importance community service plays in the college admissions process?
❏ What volunteer positions might give me some insight into career possibilities?

Helping Yourself through
Helping Others

Some high schools mandate participation in community service as a graduation requirement, integrating service into the curriculum as a learning experience. Students are graded on the service plus the connected acade-

10 Ways to Find Fun
Community Service Opportunities

❑ Hospitals are delighted to put you to work in the gift shop or library, delivering flowers or assisting patients in simple matters, such as bringing them drinking water.

❑ Any day high schoolers show up at veterans' homes, nursing homes, or hospice facilities is a good day for residents. Reading, playing games, or just talking is a gift to them. Your friendliness lingers long after the visit.

❑ Your local animal shelter always needs dog walkers and fur brushers. Maybe you'd rather train a shelter dog in the ways of good manners—making Fido or Fifi more adoptable.

❑ Places of worship love having teenagers as religious education or Sunday school teachers or assistants. If you'd prefer babysitting, the director can probably match you up with a roomful of toddlers somewhat removed from the worship area.

❑ Stuff envelopes, make phone calls, go door-to-door handing out flyers for political candidates—from your hometown mayor to U.S. senator. The experience can lead to a major in political science.

❑ Most high schools have service-oriented clubs whose members conduct food drives, become best buddies with Special Ed students, or help conduct drug prevention rallies at middle and elementary schools. And that's just for starters.

❑ Help stir up supper at a shelter. Don't like to cook? Maybe you can babysit once a week so parents can job search, hunt for an apartment, or attend a meeting.

❑ Even if you're already a big brother or big sister in real life, plenty of boys and girls clubs would like you to consider becoming a big sibling to one of the children their organization serves. If the time commitment sounds daunting, help out with after-school activities once a week.

❑ There are volunteer abroad programs, if you can't find one single opportunity in this whole country that appeals to you. Those opportunities may come with a hefty price tag for travel, however.

❑ If you're simply stumped, there's no shortage of Internet sites listing volunteer opportunities.

mic exercises. Other schools require you take a class researching volunteer opportunities in your community. Still others offer community service as an extracurricular activity, often with guidance provided by a sponsor-teacher or community member. While approaches differ, the goals are all pretty much the same: they expose students to the benefits of giving time and talent in service to others for no pay.

A government report says community service appears to be associated with more confidence in your ability to speak at public meetings and a stronger understanding of politics. But educators probably just hope you'll get hooked on the experience and remain an active volunteer and good citizen for about the next 100 years.

End-of-Chapter Questions

2.1 Why is it important to get involved in extracurricular activities, sports, and/or community service?

2.2 Why do college admissions reps look for such activities on your application? How can participating in extracurricular activities make me stand out?

2.3 What are the advantages and disadvantages of signing up for a whole bunch of activities?

2.4 What's the difference between quality and quantity of activities as far as college admissions reps are concerned?

2.5 How will I know which activities I'll like? What about the time it takes to be active?

2.6 How will I know if I'm involved in too many activities?

2.7 What should I expect to put into and get out of high school sports? What should I expect from my coach? What can I do if I don't feel the coach is treating me fairly?

2.8 Do I have to trade in my hobbies once I get busy in high school?

2.9 Why is community service part of some high schools' curricula?

2.10 How can I figure out where I fit in the world of volunteerism? What kinds of volunteer opportunities sound good to me?

3
Work and School

The United States is one of the few industrialized nations where teenagers commonly work *and* go to high school. Elsewhere, students your age go to high school. Period. In this country, approximately 80 percent of students from 16 to 18 years old work during the school year or summer. Some take part-time jobs to help support their family; some work so they can salt away paychecks for college expenses; some work so they can just buy stuff.

Betsy Downey of Consumer Credit Counseling Service of Nebraska explains, "Older teens are in the process of shifting their spending habits from childhood patterns—when they could spend any money on immediate wants—to adult patterns—when they will need to reserve some money for future expenses and emergencies. This takes time to plan and the skill of thinking into the future. For example, if your car needs repairs or you need a new prom dress, where is the money you need to spend coming from? If you spend it all as you get it, you lose the power of making choices in the future."

Most teens who work during the school year also work during the summer. But about 8 percent of students have jobs during the summer only, and that percentage is decreasing. Instead of spending three months as a lifeguard, fast-food server, or whatever, some students are opting for classes, camps, or travel. Families who can afford it often encourage their students to take additional courses, hoping these learning experiences will enhance their chances of getting into a highly selective school or receiving scholarships.

What's best for you? As with most of the decisions you'll be making en route to college, the answer is as individual as you are. Although you may want to work when you're 14 or 15 years old, the government attaches a few strings to your work plans. When school is in session (Labor Day through May 31, according to the federal government), you may work no more than three hours per school day (Monday through Friday), no more than 18 hours per week, and never before 7 a.m. or after 7 p.m. When school is out-of-session (officially June 1 to Labor Day), you may work no more than eight hours per day and no more than 40 hours per week—and never before 7 a.m. or after 9 p.m. Once you turn 16, there are no federal government restrictions about how long or what time you may work.

Pro: Get a Job

Ever notice how adults can come up with a bucketful of reasons why you should work? Some even go beyond the standard "It's good for you" or "I had a job when I was your age." Reasons that may make sense to you include:

❏ You have to help meet family expenses.

❏ College admissions representatives will look at your grades, test scores, extracurricular activities, community service, and hobbies, as well as your work experience.

❏ Having a good employee track record speaks to dependability, reliability, character, and an understanding of the importance of work. (If you have no work experiences listed on your college applications, the admissions rep may wonder why; if you believe your reasons are good, share them with the rep.)

❏ Work introduces you to the adult world and puts a realistic spin on some lessons learned in the classroom.

❏ Part-time jobs for high school students who are college bound often become a social leveler by providing experiences in the world of the working class.

❏ If you're a senior who will do anything to get out of the house, work's a viable alternative.

While a school year or summer job won't be the highlight of your career, working in a field you find interesting may provide valuable insight into professions for later on. Day care, babysitting, or work as a nanny may lead to a career in education, child psychology, or pediatrics. Retail positions might spark an interest in marketing, advertising, sales, or even design. Outdoor work—tending flower beds, mowing, basic landscape chores—can take you into horticulture.

Even if your job is on the bottom rung of the career ladder, the experience should teach money management and time management skills, as well as help you develop the ability to work with people.

School Plus a Job

Most experts say working 10 to 12 hours a week—with the majority during the weekend—is plenty during the school year. Additional hours may have a negative impact on school attendance, homework, participation in

How Much Does Uncle Sam Get?

❑ Let's say you earn $7 an hour and work 10 hours per week. You'll gross $70 per week.

❑ Of course, there are deductions: Federal Income Tax: $1.90; Social Security: $4.34; Medicare: $1.01.

❑ So your actual take-home pay is $62.75.

What about a Budget?

❑ Have I set goals for my money?

❑ Have I set up a budget to keep track of income and expenses?

❑ Have I included predictable deductions, such as for income tax, within the budget?

❑ What expenses come with this job? Clothing? Parking or other transportation costs?

❑ As I track income and expenses, what am I spending money on that falls outside the budget I established?

❑ Have I encountered unpredictable expenses, such as paying for repairs after a fender bender, and made adjustments for them?

❑ Am I putting some money in savings and watching my savings grow?

❑ Have I considered giving some to charity?

Having a Job during the School Year

I started working as a freshman. My first jobs were grocery store bagger, concession stand guy at the movie theater, then a restaurant host. From the summer before my senior year until I went to college, I worked at a retail store in sales and customer service. The other summers, I was mostly with relatives in Alaska. I didn't do many extracurricular activities as a freshman and sophomore, but played tennis junior and senior years, and took lessons outside of school. I was also Math Club president, but that wasn't very demanding. I was always involved in rock climbing and started a club at school.

My mom wanted me to have my own spending money. I'd save for a few months, then blow it on something; I don't even remember what now. Senior year, I saved some money for college books and stuff. But mostly I just spent it on rock climbing equipment, climbing trips, gas, movies, and fast food. I never made more than $8 an hour, which was decent.

At my first jobs, I would only work until 7 p.m. two or maybe three days a week and a bunch on Saturday and Sunday. It never interfered with homework or things I wanted to do. I didn't like working Friday nights. I worked at the restaurant until 9 p.m. so I stayed up later doing homework or got it done before work. Most of my jobs were never too late, which was the main factor for me. My parents watched my grades when I was working. If one grade slipped a lot, I'd start working in that class.

When you're 14 and 15, you kind of get stuck with jobs you don't like that much. If you can find something you somewhat enjoy, that's more beneficial to keeping that job. My retail job was in a climbing store. I got discounts and liked being around people with similar interests. I didn't keep any other job more than six months; it was torturous to be there.

Eric Rafferty, University of Redlands, California

school activities, and a normal social life. If you start cutting classes to catch up on your sleep, if your grades begin to slide, or if you never have an opportunity to participate in extracurricular activities or be with friends, you might consider cutting back on your work hours.

If you're a good employee, you may be asked repeatedly to put in more time on the job. (Employers ask that of dependable employees.) Don't be afraid to say, "Thanks, but no thanks." No matter what your part-time job, your first job is school.

Not Having a Job during the School Year

My parents never wanted me to work during the school year; they wanted me to do school work. I played lacrosse freshman and sophomore years, but after I stopped playing sports, there was more and more homework. Classes got harder, and I started taking higher-level classes. Applying to college was a really long, tedious process, so I had very little time to do anything. As a senior, I was president of our school's Shaker Heights Project Support Club, a social club that worked with students [in the regular curriculum] and students who were developmentally handicapped. We did something once a month. On weekends, I wanted to relax with friends.

None of my close friends had like real jobs during the school year. Most of us babysat. I used that for spending money, and my parents would pay for most of my stuff.

My parents encouraged me to work during the summer; they didn't want me just sitting around doing nothing. And you go out so much more during the summer and spend so much more. For the first three years, I worked for a month as a counselor at a summer overnight camp. I was responsible for a cabin of little girls and was a lifeguard and did arts and crafts. The summer after graduation, I babysat full-time.

I'm not working in college. I have less time here than in high school.

The decision to work during high school often depends upon your financial situation. If you need to have that extra money and you feel like you can balance a job and academics, go for it. If you don't need a job and aren't good at time management, stay clear of it. But work in the summers so you'll have money to go out to dinner and things. Otherwise, you'll get bored.

Lauren LaMalfa, University of Indiana, Bloomington

Con: Don't Get a Job

Not everyone is anxious to see you trot off to work after the school day ends. Research indicates the more hours a student works, the fewer hours the student studies. Students who work 15 or more hours a week show a decline in grades and perform less well on standardized tests. They're less likely to take more demanding courses, particularly in higher-level math and science. In fact, when a high percentage of students in a school hold part-time jobs, teachers begin to lower their expectations for performance and, in turn, students learn less. Besides impinging on academics, time at work means time away from building friendships and exploring new interests.

School as a Job

Some parents say that school *is* their student's job—at least during the school year. Jim Adams's three children only worked in the summer. "We nixed working during the school year, even though the kids didn't have as many things as their friends," he says. "We felt they'd spend most of their earnings on stuff they didn't need to be happy. Their real job was school—tough classes and activities. Some days they'd be at school at 6 a.m. and not back home until 7 p.m. Then, they had homework. It took more commitment than a full-time job. Our children were learning social and leadership skills. And they were so busy and tired, they didn't even need a curfew."

Balancing Work and School

If you combine a positive work environment with continuing success at school, a part-time job can be beneficial, not stressful. That means realistic work hours, an orderly workplace, clear work assignments, mature supervision, and the opportunity to learn valuable lessons. It also means achieving grade expectations, selecting challenging courses, and having time for extracurricular activities, a social life, and, perhaps, volunteer opportunities.

Is This Job Worth It?

- ❏ Will I be able to accomplish my long-term financial goals with this job?
- ❏ Can I earn a sufficient income to justify expenses incurred by merely having the job?
- ❏ Am I learning job skills and people skills?
- ❏ Do I look forward to or dread going to work?
- ❏ Am I maintaining good grades? Participating in extracurricular activities? Do I still have a social life?
- ❏ Does my boss or supervisor make adjustments for my school schedule?
- ❏ Would I be better off looking for another job or not working?
- ❏ Has working helped me learn the difference between my needs and my wants?

End-of-Chapter Questions

3.1 What are good reasons for having a job during the school year? Do those reasons describe my situation?

3.2 What are the federal government's restrictions on how much I can work when I'm in school? Why are limits imposed?

3.3 How can I tell if I'm working too many hours? How can I measure if it's worth my time to work?

3.4 Have I thought about the difference between how much I earn and how much I bring home?

3.5 If I get a job, why should I create a budget? Realistically, would I save some money?

3.6 What are good reasons for not having a job during the school year? Do those reasons describe my situation?

3.7 What about working during the school year and summer? What about working only in the summer?

3.8 Why are some students opting not to work in the summer? Would those reasons apply in my situation?

3.9 What does it take to have a job and do well in school?

4
Primer on College Costs

There's one given for college costs: They've been skyrocketing and are expected to continue to go up, up, up. Nevertheless, even if you just realized that college costs a hunk of money, and you don't have a money tree or rich aunt, you and your family still have many financial options to help you become a college graduate.

Once you get past the initial shock and consider the lifelong investment the education represents, you can figure a strategy to pay for college. Enlist help from your high school guidance counselor, college financial aid officers at each school in which you are interested (financial aid is a different department from admissions), federal and state government financial aid representatives, and your family tax advisor or financial planner. In addition, Internet sites ranging from government to not-for-profit to commercial are packed full of information. Basic costs are tuition and room and board. Additionally, you have books, personal items, transportation home, and other costs that are difficult to predict precisely but are there.

Tuition and Room and Board

Tuition (including fees) varies from about $1,000 to more than $30,000. Then you add room and board, which rings up about $10,000 at some private schools. Private Vanderbilt University in Nashville, Tennessee, charges about $28,400 for tuition and another $9,400 for room and board. These costs are usually much less at state institutions. For example, the University of Tennessee in Knoxville charges about $4,400 for tuition and room and board for Tennessee residents and about $13,500 for out-of-state students. Southwest Tennessee Community College in Memphis charges about $1,000 in-state tuition and $3,800 for out-of-state students. As a non-residential school, Southwest Tennessee has no room and board charges, but students who do not commute will have their own living expenses.

One more cost fact: Southwest Tennessee has an agreement (called an articulation agreement) with Southern Illinois University-Carbondale that the community college credits earned for the associate's degree will transfer to SIUC toward a bachelor's degree. In-state tuition at SIUC is about $5,500 and out-of state $9,800. Taking core courses for two years at Southwest Tennessee can be a significant savings. (SIU's Web page, www.regis trar.siu.edu/eval/articpg.htm, lists all the schools, with links to the specific courses SIU accepts.)

Other Costs

Books

Believe it—some books cost $90! And some paperback novels for English literature cost $15. Figure four or five classes and at least one book per class. Check online for used books. Get to the campus bookstore early for used books, but skip the ones that have highlighted text, since that will prove distracting when you study. Some schools offer loans of used textbooks for students on financial aid.

Personal

Colleges will suggest a figure, often based on an average from student surveys. Only you know how much you might spend on items such as laundry or room decor (wastebasket, lamp, curtains, bedspread, rug, maybe a loft bed, bath towel, sheets, and so the dollars dribble away).

Travel

Transportation between college and home can be simple if you are two hours away. If you are halfway across the country, though, you're looking at more significant costs for train or plane fares or for your vehicle cost and maintenance. Check with transportation companies for special deals for students, and make sure they can be used during the holidays. Also, check your final exam schedule early in the semester so you can purchase tickets early at less cost.

Study Abroad

At some schools one-third of the students spend part or all of their junior year studying and exploring the culture of a foreign country. Costs may be about the same as being on campus, but that's not a given. Check for other programs that might be less expensive than your school's; see whether your financial aid applies to study abroad; and find out if you will still have enough credits to graduate in four years. One student found a program allowing him to study in Freiberg, Germany, paying the same cost as German students—about $600 instead of the $18,000 annual tuition at his private college. His parents missed him but wished they could send him for his senior year too!

Summer Classes

If classes get closed out for the school year, you may have to take summer classes to graduate on time. Tuition does not include summer school. And it may be hard to work while you are in class and studying. Conversely, you may be able to take enough summer classes to finish a semester or two early and bring in a livable salary, making the extra summer school costs worthwhile.

Insurance

You may need insurance for your laptop, desktop computer, stereo equipment, and other possessions. Also, ask your family insurance agent about how much insurance will cost if you plan to have a car at school. Some insurers offer discounts with proof of good grades.

Health Insurance

College students are notorious for keeping funny hours, not eating right, and generally getting stressed out. So, when you're sick, does the family insurance pay fees for the health center, doctor, or, if necessary, the hospital emergency room? Is the college's health insurance plan better than the family's? Does the college offer insurance so that if you are too ill to continue, you receive credit or a refund of the semester's tuition? Does your family insurance even cover a student away from home? One Florida family found their son was not covered when he went to college in a different Florida county.

Spring Break

No kidding. Trips to sunny climes eat into college funds, and financial aid definitely doesn't apply.

Technology

Most schools recommend that students have a computer. Your school may have a deal with one manufacturer so you can get a discount if you purchase that brand. Many students also have a cell phone, so find the best deals for minutes and to avoid roaming charges.

Food

Despite signing up for breakfast, lunch, and dinner, you're not going to make every meal. Then you have to pay extra at the dining hall, buy groceries, eat out, or order pizza delivery. Or hope your parents send you that overdue care package or show up to take you and your friends out for dinner.

Who Will Pay for What: Options That Work

One part of the equation for funding a college education is the dialogue between you and your parents. It's not unusual for this dialogue to never occur or to occur sometime during your senior year. On the other hand, some parents sit down at the kitchen table with their youngsters in eighth grade and talk about responsibilities, options, and financial and other consequences for every member of the family, excluding the dog. The result of the dialogue should be an understanding of who pays for what for college—and how.

How to split college costs is as variable as individual families. At one end of the spectrum are parents who can and will pay for everything. At the other end sit parents who cannot or will not pay for anything. Somewhere in between are parents and students who share the costs in various ways.

Some parents pay tuition, fees, room and board; the student is responsible for all spending money. Others pay everything for four years and if the student does not graduate then, the student will pay the rest. Janet Heimbuch told her daughter the amount the family would contribute each year for college. When the daughter realized there was a gap between family financing and the colleges she was investigating, she turned

Calculate Your Costs

Go to www.finaid.org/calculators/ for calculators for everything to do with financing college. Basically, you'll be able to figure how much college will cost, how much you'll need to save, and how much aid you'll get. (Don't throw the computer out the window when you find out!) According to the site, the most popular calculators are the College Cost Projector, Savings Plan Designer, Expected Family Contribution, and Financial Aid Calculator.

You'll need some data to effectively use the calculators. The College Cost Projector, for example, needs to use the total figure now for attendance, including tuition, fees, room and board, books, travel, and incidental expenses for any school in which you're interested. Check school Web sites or call the financial aid offices because this information is at their fingertips. You also enter the number of years before you attend college. The calculator will figure your yearly and total amount. Be aware, though, that these totals are not indelibly written. Always check with college financial aid offices.

Eight Ways to Save Dollars

1. Try to earn course credit through AP classes and exams in high school or CLEP tests.
2. Take core classes at a community college that has agreements with four-year colleges to accept the credits.
3. Take heavier course loads than the 12-hour minimum for full-time students.
4. Keep track of your finances and watch the discretionary expenses.
5. Limit your credit card debt.
6. Work while you are in college.
7. Buy used books. Sell those you won't need again.
8. Consider serving in the National Guard or ROTC for financial aid in return for service commitment.

her attention to state schools where she would not have to take out loans to pay the difference.

Loans and who is responsible should be a hot topic. Everyone needs to understand the cost of any loans and how long it will take to be debt-free. Also, unpaid student loans can wreak havoc on the credit ratings. One family agreed the students would sign for any loans available in their financial aid packages. The students were in their thirties when they finished payments, but they said they would not have had the same job opportunities had they attended their state college.

Those financial choices also include lifestyle consequences for students and families. For some, cutting back or living sparsely is not a hardship; for others, changing lifestyle is untenable. Know your limits and figure out what works for you and your parents.

While money is a big issue, it's not the only issue. With parental and an independent college consultant's full agreement, Jay Welch's son ignored the total living environment and chose to go to the college that had offered a great scholarship. He transferred after two years. "It was totally wrong for him. We went back to our own parameters for the next child," says Welch.

Financial Aid Primer

Here's a lesser known truth about college tuition: not everyone pays the same at the same institution. That's because colleges "buy" students through awarding financial aid. Although colleges don't want to sound like big-box discount stores, they do allocate merit aid to meet institutional goals. For instance, a generous scholarship can entice a Florida football player away from his home-state colleges, or a top scholar to a less prestigious institution than the Ivies. Such merit awards ultimately may lead to higher rankings in the *U.S. News* annual survey, which, in turn, leads to more and better qualified applicants overall.

Here's another truth: financial aid is no longer solely for indigent families. With the rising cost of tuition and room and board, many so-called middle-class families apply for and receive aid. Indeed, it is not unusual for families with incomes of more than $100,000 to receive aid.

Such financial aid is not all free money, however. Much is in the form of loans that you and your family must repay. If you have filled out the appropriate financial aid applications, colleges issue a financial aid package once you are admitted. The package may be comprised of scholarships and grants (no repayment needed), loans, and work-study funds. You may refuse any part of the package, but the amount you must come up with through loans and work-study remains the same. For federal student aid, check www. studentaid.ed.gov/PORTALSWebApp/students/english/index.jsp.

How Much Debt Is Too Much?

❏ What responsibilities do I have or expect to have as I'm paying back college loans?

❏ Have I calculated how long it will take me to pay off the loans?

❏ Have I consulted with a financial advisor or college financial aid officer for realistic projections and debt amounts?

❏ Do I have any thoughts about going to graduate school, which will likely amass further debts?

❏ How frugally can I stand to live?

Compare various lenders for borrower benefits and repayment terms. As with a house or car loan, look for the best value. Understand what fees are deducted from your loan and if the lender has repayment incentives.

Your financial aid package may not cover all your expenses, even when you take out the maximum loans allowed. In that case, contact your financial aid office about options at that school.

FAFSA

Before you can qualify for any federal, state, or college financial aid, you must fill out the FAFSA. There is no fee to apply for student aid, but it usually takes more time to fill out than seeing a movie. You need to provide your income, net worth, federal tax return information, family size, and number of family members in college. Children of divorced parents need to ask a college financial aid officer about what is required from both parents and any stepparents. Paper FAFSAs are available in your counselor's office and college financial aid offices.

But the fastest, most accurate way to file your FAFSA is on the Web at www.fafsa.ed.gov. You can file electronically with or without a PIN—Personal Identification Number. The PIN serves as an electronic signature. You may use the same PIN every year as you renew your FAFSA. However, if you submit electronically without the student's and/or parent's PIN, you must print, sign, and mail the signature page as soon as possible. With a PIN, enter the parent's PIN after you submit the FAFSA. You may have to return to the main Web site and use the "Provide an Electronic Signature" button.

Key Terms to Know

Private scholarships: do not repay; awards for outstanding academics, financial need, community service, and/or special groups.

College scholarships and grants: do not repay; awards for special talents and financial need.

FAFSA (Free Application for Federal Student Aid): required for any federal financial aid as well as most private aid.

Federal Pell Grant: do not repay; need-based.

FSEOG (Federal Supplemental Educational Opportunity Grant): do not repay; need-based.

Federal Work Study: must work, usually on campus at jobs paying at least minimum wage; need-based.

Federal Perkins Loan: repay; need-based.

Stafford Loan: major source for need- and non-need-based self-help aid.

FFELP (Federal Family Education Loan Program) Stafford Loan: loans from commercial banks, credit unions, and savings banks. You get an application from the lender or your college financial aid office.

Direct (William D. Ford Federal Direct Loan Program) Stafford Loan: U.S. Department of Education loans the money to the student through the college.

Direct and FFELP PLUS Loan: parent is borrower.

Subsidized loan: need-based; no interest until repayment begins; repayment grace period of six months after graduation or changing to less than half-time student status.

Unsubsidized loan: non-need-based; interest is due while in school and during the six-month grace period, but can be postponed.

If you provide an e-mail address, within a week (versus four weeks for paper FAFSAs) you will receive an e-mail with a link to your Student Aid Report (SAR). The link will expire after 14 days if you don't use it, but SARs can be accessed anytime with the student's PIN.

File your FAFSA as soon as possible after January 1 of the year you will attend college. If the family's tax information is not completely available, file estimated figures to get the process moving. You can make corrections later, if needed. Also, be aware of the college's priority deadline. Much financial aid goes on a first-come, first-served basis, so you want to get in before the piggy bank is empty.

The Student Aid Report indicates your Expected Family Contribution: how much you and your family "are expected to contribute" based on complicated formulae at the U.S. Department of Education. You and your family will probably be convinced you can't possibly pay that amount and the FAFSA people must have made an error. Not so. That contribution really means what you are able to pay in terms of your assets and borrowing capability. The Student Aid Report never says a family is not eligible for financial aid.

Many schools also require that a simpler financial aid application be submitted with your admission application. You probably can fill it out yourself. Colleges download your Expected Family Contribution and subtract that EFC from the school's costs for tuition, books, fees, and living expenses to determine your eligibility for scholarships, grants, loans, and work-study in a financial aid package.

Faster FAFSA

Follow these steps:

1. Go to www.pin.ed.gov to get a Personal Identification Number (PIN). You and your parent must have separate PIN numbers. Fill in your name, Social Security number, birth date, and address. E-mail address is optional but you'll get your PIN faster. Order your PINs at least two weeks before completing the FAFSA.

2. Go to www.fafsa.ed.gov to fill out the application. To save online time, you may want to fill out the paper version from your counselor's office as a draft and then copy the information to the online FAFSA.

3. Follow instructions for submitting your parent's PIN, which acts as an electronic signature.

Your package will vary from one college to the other, so compare and ask questions of the financial aid officers. Schools do have some flexibility and may make some adjustments to your expected contribution. Some students have been able to negotiate better packages.

CSS/Financial Aid Profile

Many schools use information from this profile, a service of the College Board (www.collegeboard.com), to award nonfederal student aid. Your profile is sent to colleges you specify. It enables you to give a complete picture of your family's financial situation, including any special circumstances.

Register for the Financial Aid Profile online or by telephone for a paper application. Applying online saves a couple dollars, but have your credit card handy for the registration fee plus a fee for each school you list as a recipient. Check with your high school counselor for fee waivers based on income level. If needed, you can download and print the Business/Farm Supplement or Noncustodial Parent's Statement. Submit the profile at least one week before your colleges' priority filing date, which you can find by clicking on the CSS/Profile home page. If you complete your profile application online, you will receive an online acknowledgment.

Other Financial Aid Sources

AmeriCorps is a national service program in which people work in communities in education, the environment, human interaction, and public safety in return for financial assistance for postsecondary training. Applicants must be at least 17 and be willing to work 1,700 hours for one year. Upon completion of the commitment, participants receive $4,725 as either a tuition voucher or repayment of an outstanding student loan.

Veterans Administration and Vocational Rehabilitation Programs may offer college aid to qualified students. Supplemental aid may be available for children of deceased or disabled veterans. Check with your state's veterans affairs department as well as college financial aid offices and your guidance counselor.

Some states have forgivable loan programs. The Iowa Teacher Shortage Forgivable Loan Program, for instance, forgives up to $9,000 of Iowa resident students' loans in return for a commitment to teach five years in an area of Iowa that has a teacher shortage. There's a similar program for nurses. Once again, check with college financial aid offices or do an Internet search.

Tax Information Sites to Know

Your higher education costs and financing may be eligible for tax credits and deductions. There are also education savings accounts (formerly known as Education IRAs) and college savings plans, also known as 529 Plans, set up by individual states. Separate rules apply to each plan. Always check with your tax advisor or financial planner to understand your situation. The following sites give detailed descriptions of tax benefits and savings plans options:

❏ www.nasfaa.org/annualpubs/taxbenefitsguide.pdf: Parent and Student Guide to Federal Tax Benefits for Tuition and Fees

❏ www.irs.gov/pub/irs-pdf/p970.pdf: Publication 970 (PDF), Tax Benefits for Education

❏ www.irs.gov/faqs/index.html: Frequently Asked Tax Questions and Answers, Education Tax Credits

Some colleges offer campus-specific discounts to get students to take classes during off-peak hours or in the summer. For students who take classes after 3 p.m. and at 8 and 8:30 a.m., the University of Oregon offers a 15 percent reduction. Check with the financial aid office for the year you intend to enroll.

If government loans don't meet all your needs, work with your parents to take out private loans in their names. Parents likely can get a more favorable interest rate with a PLUS loan. Of course, there are many reasons parents do not want to take out the PLUS loans. They figure the student must have ownership of his or her education; they're willing to pay for public but not private college; or the student missed the deadline for FAFSA filing and must suffer the consequences.

End-of-Chapter Questions

4.1 What items make up basic college costs? Am I keeping track for schools in which I'm interested?

4.2 Should I use the Internet to find cost information?

4.3 Do I understand the tuition cost differences between state and private institutions? Between four-year colleges and two-year community colleges?

4.4 How will I know if any community college credits will transfer to a particular four-year institution?

4.5 Have I checked costs for plane tickets and other travel? Does studying abroad sound exciting? How do I investigate costs?

4.6 Will my family's health insurance cover me at college? Do I need to purchase the college's health insurance plan?

4.7 What information do I need to perform online calculations for projected college costs?

4.8 What is the FAFSA? Is there a fee?

4.9 Is the FAFSA only for students below a certain income level?

4.10 When can I send in the FAFSA? Will I get a FAFSA decision faster online or by sending a paper application?

4.11 What's included in the Student Aid Report?

4.12 What if our Expected Family Contribution is too big?

4.13 Do colleges and the government expect me to pay for part of my tuition even if I qualify for financial aid?

4.14 Do I understand the parts of a financial aid package? Must I accept all parts of the financial aid package? Is it appropriate to negotiate with schools about financial aid packages?

4.15 Should I choose a college based on the best financial aid package?

5
Scholarships and Managing Money

Scholarships and grants are free money—you don't have to pay back the organization or college that gave you the award. Scholarships are generally from organizations and companies; grants are usually issued by governments and colleges. The awards may be need- or merit-based. There's one catch: you have to earn these awards by being a good citizen, taking challenging high school classes, developing your interests and strengths, researching available scholarships, and, finally, applying for them.

Searching for Scholarships

The Web site www.fastweb.com is widely used and recommended. After 20 minutes of answering questions and clicking "No" to offers for other commercial information, a list of 62 scholarships matched our test profile. Many matches were national essay writing contests and dot-com sponsored awards or contests; others included labor union, regional, and state awards. You might find a great opportunity, but don't use just one list as your sole search for free money.

Where Should I Look?

- ❏ Start locally. Ask your high school guidance counselor and chamber of commerce for lists of local scholarship offers.

- ❏ Ask professional, religious, or social organizations to which you, your parents, or a relative belong.

- ❏ Have your parents ask at work. Some employers offer scholarships to employees' children or tuition reimbursement programs. Unions may offer scholarships to members and their children.

- ❏ Check with college financial aid offices. They have access to computer databases and often have a list of scholarship and grant options. Also check with the department in your major area of study and college Web sites.

- ❏ Use library computers to search databases and find books on how to find free money for college.

- ❏ Do Internet searches in each database by modifying your personal characteristics or profile.

- ❏ Check state and federal grant programs. To begin, ask your counselor for application materials and procedures.

Seven Ways to Maximize Your Chances for Free College Money

1. Apply for local scholarships. They will probably be considerably less than big-deal national scholarships, but fewer people will be applying.

2. Your best bet for big money will come from the college you choose to attend because that scholarship is most likely renewable each year.

3. The more scholarships you apply for, the more you're likely to receive.

4. If an essay is required, there'll be fewer applicants paddling around in the scholarship pool.

5. Search out scholarships that reward a good student who hasn't already won other scholarships.

6. Be flexible in considering your choice of colleges because one might offer you a better deal than the next. Even so, don't compromise your opportunity for an excellent education.

7. Skip long applications that yield little money.

Scholarship Scams

You do not need to pay anyone to find scholarships for you. That's because you have the same access as any business to the databases. Even so, people do pay because they don't have time to search or the confidence that they will be thorough. And sometimes people get taken in by fraudulent companies involved in scams.

When you get scammed, you lose your hard-earned bucks for college and get little or nothing in return. Recognizing that fraud occurs regularly, the Federal Trade Commission (FTC) and U.S. Department of Education have increased consumer education. Parents and students can heed these red flags: guarantees of scholarships in return for advance fees, a money-back guarantee but with conditions that make it impossi-

10 Mistakes to Avoid

1. Going it alone instead of making the process a team effort involving family, guidance counselor, and mentor(s).

2. Trying to wing the college entrance tests.

3. Remaining convinced that your position as center on the basketball team will net you a full-ride scholarship, and not applying yourself academically or looking for other scholarships.

4. Using reference guides that are three years old and ignoring the Internet.

5. Not reading the guidelines and applying for scholarships for which you do not qualify.

6. Tiring of the process and neglecting to search for scholarships others may have overlooked.

7. Procrastinating until it's too late for you to rewrite and polish your essay.

8. Wearing jeans to the interview, slouching, and chewing gum. (Or any one of those three.)

9. Keeping all your scholarship information, applications, and recommendations in one big pile on the floor. Successful applicants develop a plan—and follow it.

10. Walking into the counseling office on deadline day and, without prior notice, expecting transcripts and letters of recommendation to be ready.

FTC Warning: Watch Out for These Lines

❏ "This scholarship is guaranteed or your money back."

❏ "You can't get this information anywhere else."

❏ "I just need your credit card or bank account number to hold this scholarship."

❏ "We'll do all the work."

❏ "This scholarship will cost some money."

❏ "You've been selected by a national foundation to receive a scholarship." Or, "You're a finalist" in a contest you did not enter.

ble to get the refund, and notification you are a "finalist" for awards that require an up-front fee. Sometimes these companies request the student's checking account number to confirm eligibility and then debit the account without the student's consent. Or, companies quote a small weekly or monthly fee and request that you allow them to debit your account for an unlimited time. Beware of unsolicited offers by phone, e-mail, or regular mail.

Still, the FTC says there are legitimate companies that say they can get a list of scholarships for an advance fee. The difference between legitimate and scam companies is that the legitimate companies never promise or guarantee you will be awarded the scholarships or grants they show you as available.

If you suspect you are enmeshed in a scam, file a complaint at www.ftc.gov or call toll-free 1-877-FTC-HELP (1-877-382-4357); TTY (telecommunications device for the deaf): 1-866-653-4261.

Personal Money Management 101

How you manage your money in college will make a big difference in how well you live after college. If you indulge nearly all your "wants" in college and pile up loans and credit card debts, you'll need to land an investment banker's high-flying salary immediately or live frugally when you join the real world and pay off your debts, which could take years.

Attention Parents: 10 Ways to Help
Your Student Win Scholarships

1. Avoid the urge to take over, even when you know best.

2. Ask your student how you can be most helpful in the process. Maybe it's just addressing envelopes or taking the application to the post office.

3. Ask your student what the deadlines are and then mark them on your calendar too. When they come close, you can offhandedly ask if any deadlines are coming up.

4. When push comes to shove (and it will), lighten up on your student's household responsibilities till everything is in the mail.

5. If you are asked to read the essay, suggest changes tactfully by asking questions leading to clarification or reorganization of ideas.

6. Never, ever, do the applications for your student. It's okay to fill in some routine information blanks, but not sections that require sentences. And certainly not the essay.

7. Discuss the idea of rejection up front. Competition is stiff and rejection isn't personal, but that's hard to believe after your student's hard work. Pursue enough scholarships and it's likely that your student will get some free money.

8. Discuss family finances to help your youngster understand how free money may impact the choice of schools. If some schools must be ruled out—no matter how much scholarship money is possible—discuss that early in the process.

9. Get online yourself to become knowledgeable about scholarship opportunities. The more you know, the better you can work with your student.

10. Be patient, listen, and offer suggestions when asked.

Even if you have done well managing your allowance or after-school job earnings with your own bank account and credit card, money seems to fly out the window at college. Parent Joyce Pope's daughter worked all summer to save $1,000 for her college spending money for concerts, university sweatshirts, and more. With three weeks remaining in her spring semester, the first-year student called home for funds to replenish her depleted bank account. Pope says, "I sent her the only two things I thought she really needed: Tampax and toothpaste." Next time her daughter called home, she had a waitress job while studying for finals, and the young woman had solved the problem herself, as her mother wanted her to do.

The basics for managing your college money are fairly simple. Open a bank account, write a budget for what you think costs will be, and avoid credit card debt.

Opening Your Bank Account

You may open a bank account in your new college town during orientation. Financial institutions will have representatives and information available and are used to dealing with new students. Alternatively, you may access your hometown checking account through ATM machines. That might make it easy for Mom or Dad to replenish your account. But compare fees for items such as checks and ATM use. Will you need to pay $1 or more every time you do an ATM withdrawal or deposit?

Also, balance that checking account monthly to make sure you still have enough money in your account to cover your costs and to note where the money has gone. If most of the entries are for miscellaneous ATM withdrawals, it's time to compare spending with your budget projections.

Create Your Budget

Making a budget to guide spending is never at the top of anyone's fun-things-to-do list. But it's still the best way to figure out how much money you need to live on and if you are spending your money as you want to. To make a budget, track your current spending, evaluate that spending to set spending guidelines, and, finally, track your spending to ensure that you stay within those guidelines. Ask your parents for current costs for basic needs and wants.

Managing Debt

It's so easy to get in over your head with debts in college. One way to manage debt is to pay interest as it accrues in college on unsubsidized federal and private loans. For example, for a loan of $15,000 at 8.25 percent interest, if you pay the interest while in college, you will pay approximately $17 less per month after college as you repay the loan. That's about $1,987 less over the lifetime of the loan, which will go far toward a cool sound system.

A growing problem is students' credit card debt. Students are bombarded with credit card offers the moment they step on campus, if not before. Those companies know that students spend a lot of dollars and have good potential earning power.

How Much Will I Spend at College?

❏ How much do my clothes and personal items for one year cost?

❏ Do I prefer to cook for myself or subscribe to a dining hall plan?

❏ How often do I eat pizza with my friends now? Go to movies or other entertainment?

❏ Will I have formal events to attend, fraternity or sorority fees, or other social expenses?

❏ Have I checked out a college bookstore to see how much new and used textbooks cost?

❏ Will I have a vehicle at college? What are fees for insurance and parking? How often have I had to get the vehicle repaired, and is that pattern likely to continue? Will I need snow tires if I'm from Georgia and going to college in the Northeast?

❏ Will I be able to hitch a ride home with someone or will I have to purchase bus, train, or plane tickets? How much are those fares during the holidays when I'll want to get home?

❏ If I break an arm playing intramurals and go to the emergency room, does my health insurance (either through family or the college) cover that expense?

Fast Facts about Credit Cards

❏ 77 percent of full-time undergraduates have credit cards.

❏ 20 percent have four or more cards.

❏ 59 percent pay their balances in full and on time most months.

❏ The average outstanding balance per student is $2,226.

❏ 20 percent of students at four-year schools carry debt of at least $10,000 by graduation.

❏ Every card is worth $600 to $1,000 clear profit to the issuing company.

Overwhelmed by
Credit Card Debts

Credit card offers have arrived in the mail—probably about three a week— ever since I was a freshman. I got my first credit card when I was 22, as a sophomore at another college. (I took a year off, then I had to take a year of noncredit classes and I also changed my major a few times.) The offer was sent unsolicited in the mail, and my dad thought it would be a good idea if I got a credit card to get a good credit rating.

At first I had a good paying job and could pay the bills. By then I had two credit cards. I charged a lot of clothes and food. I was like addicted to shopping. Then I transferred here to school and couldn't get a job that paid as well. I had money saved, but not enough to pay off the credit cards. So I got in trouble by not being able to make monthly payments on time.

I owed about $400 on one card and $600 on the other. My credit limit on the $400 one was $1,000, and on the $600 one it was $300. That bill got to $600 because they kept adding about $50 in various penalty charges each month. It took me about two months to figure out I had a problem. The $400 card started calling about the bill. They were really understanding and tried to work out a payment schedule with me.

I didn't tell my parents right away because I wanted to take care of it myself. My mom paid off the first bill and then Dad found out and paid off the second one. He was mad at me because I didn't tell him and those extra charges kept adding on. I cancelled both credit cards and am paying back my parents. I'm glad they helped me.

I'd suggest that before you get a credit card, you make sure you have a good job and have enough to pay off the monthly minimum. Also, get a credit limit for what's reasonable for your income.

Melissa Dunning, Florida State University, Tallahassee

Credit cards are so convenient to use that people forget they are high interest loans rather than real money. You add to the loan each time you use the card—for dinner out, concert tickets, gas, spring break plane tickets, books, clothes, CDs—and pretty soon you've amassed a bigger bill than you can pay. So you pay the minimum amount required and figure to pay it down monthly, which can take years. For example, for a bill of $1,500, if you pay the minimum $22 each month, you'll finish paying that particu-

Credit Card Comparisons

The Web site www.CardWeb.com allows you to compare cards in various categories: student, no annual fee, rewards (travel, gas, cash), low rate, low introductory promotional rate, and more. Comparisons are in easy-to-read charts.

The site www.bankrate.com also offers comparisons (and a lot of pop-up advertisements!) in charts with details on the rules.

Individual companies such as Citibank and American Express list their card options.

---

lar bill in 17-plus years. You'll have paid $3,124 in interest and, altogether, $4,624 for that original $1,500 bill.

Credit cards can be useful if you use them judiciously. Shop around for the best deal; compare terms and fees before you open the account; keep copies of sales slips to compare with your monthly bill; and don't choose a credit card to get a free T-shirt. One more tip: note how long you have to pay the bill. Many cards have shortened the time to 20 days from the billing date, not from when you receive the bill. That means you need to pay promptly so it can be credited to your account within the 20 days. Some companies take five to seven days to credit a payment. So you can incur late fees and interest payments quickly if you put off settling your account.

End-of-Chapter Questions

5.1 Who awards scholarships and grants?

5.2 How do I find out about scholarship opportunities? Which scholarships am I most likely to get?

5.3 Do I need to pay back scholarship and grant awards?

5.4 Should I sign up for a credit card? Do I have the necessary income to pay the bill each month? How can I compare credit card fees?

5.5 Do I know how to make a budget?

5.6 What are the advantages of having a credit card? What are the pitfalls of having a credit card?

5.7 What should I do if I can't pay my credit card bills?

6
"I Am So Stressed Out!"

Ever heard people say they were stressed out? Ever said that yourself? Most high schoolers would have to answer yes. (Wouldn't we all!)

As a high school student you're continually reminded that your future depends upon how well you perform academically. Plus, maybe you're one of those students who takes AP and Honors classes, is involved in at least one sport, has at least one extracurricular activity—perhaps through your school or community—holds down a part-time job, all while trying to get along with the family as well as your friends and the latest love of your life.

Or you might be a student whose grades are average, has chosen not to participate in activities, is quiet, isn't convinced of being college material, and hasn't connected with teachers beyond the classroom. Or maybe you're somewhere in between.

No matter. Like everyone else your age, the competition for peer approval and your growing independence from parents induce self-doubt. Plus, high school counselors keep talking about how much time and effort any college search process will take. That is a lot to handle, which is why you announce to no one and everyone, "I AM SO STRESSED OUT!"

What Is Stress?

All those things going on in your life aren't stress. They are the situations that *cause* stress. Actual stress is your body's response to any demand made on it. Common physical symptoms of stress include muscular tension, colds as well as medically unexplained aches and pains, fatigue, and headaches. Common emotional symptoms include irritability, anger, agitation, and feeling overwhelmed. Common cognitive symptoms include inability to make decisions, forgetfulness, and difficulty concentrating.

When your heart starts racing as Coach announces your basketball team's starting line-up, or when you're awake all night thinking about that half-done term paper, or when you start pacing the floor because your ride to school is late, your body is responding to demands being made upon it.

Surprisingly, there's positive stress as well as negative stress. The latter used to be called "distress," but today stress and distress are synonymous. And most people see it all as negative. Not so. Some stress is simply a part of everyday life. Positive stress, for example, motivates, improves performance, and sharpens the mind. That's the kind of stress you experience if you win the United States Academic Decathlon, for example, or learn you've been admitted to the college you wanted to go to more than anything else in the whole world. Positive stress events may be so powerful that the high is followed by a period of letdown and fatigue—which you also feel after messing up on a final exam because you didn't study. And that, of course, is negative stress.

Tension in a high schooler's life has been blamed for everything from cheating on tests to binge drinking and the ultimate negative effect—suicide. Schedules crammed with unwieldy amounts of academic classes and extracurricular activities can take a toll on your physical, mental, and emotional well-being.

At Lynbrook High School in San Jose, California, teachers are encouraged to give meaningful homework rather than busywork, provide clear expectations, and indicate how long assignments should take. They are discouraged from giving homework over weekends or holiday periods. Tutorial periods twice a week also enable students to meet during the day with teachers for help, work on projects with other students, and use the library or computer lab—something many can't do after school because of extracurricular activities or sports. Additionally, the students put on an annual stress-free week that includes jumping on a trampoline!

Stress Relievers

While your body tolerates some stress, realize that stress builds if left unaddressed. In fact, continual exposure will lower your ability to cope effectively. Left unchecked long enough, you can become physically ill and enter into a serious depression. That's why knowing how to recognize and manage your stress is so important.

What Causes Stress?

- ❏ Change and adjusting to change
- ❏ Decisions that are tough to make
- ❏ School, including classes, grades, classmates, extracurricular activities, and sports
- ❏ Homework and tests
- ❏ Relationships with friends, and with a girlfriend or boyfriend
- ❏ Searching for, applying to, and getting accepted into college
- ❏ Moving or changing schools
- ❏ Family problems such as separation or divorce of your parents, abuse, chronic illness, the death of a loved one, financial difficulties
- ❏ Living in an unsafe home or neighborhood or world
- ❏ Physical changes in your body, especially as they relate to developing a new self-image
- ❏ Unrealistically high expectations
- ❏ Concerns about safe sex, unplanned pregnancy, sexually transmitted diseases
- ❏ Violence, drinking, drugs

Seeking Help

You need to recognize the symptoms of stress and deal with the issues that are causing it. Sounds simple, but sometimes it's actually impossible. There may be times when you do everything in your power and still can't get things under control. Then you may need to seek professional help.

Perhaps the idea comes in the form of a suggestion from a teacher, your counselor, the family doctor, a friend, or a parent. Some people—not just teenagers—balk at the idea of getting professional help for stress. But look at it this way: If you fall off the sofa and break your arm, you'd go to the doctor, right? If you get a toothache that won't quit, you'd go to the dentist, right? So if you can't handle the stress in your life, why would you not go to someone trained in that area?

How Do I Handle Stress?

❏ Am I able to identify the source or sources of my stress so I know where to direct my efforts?

❏ What about relaxation exercises such as abdominal breathing and muscle relaxation techniques?

❏ Do I feel less stressed when I do a good job of organizing my time? Effective personal organization helps manage stress.

❏ Is there a network of friends who can help me cope in a positive way? What about a teacher, coach, family member, or religious advisor?

❏ Do I eat well, get enough sleep, and exercise regularly? Do I avoid excess caffeine, which can increase feelings of anxiety and agitation?

❏ Do I take a break from stressful situations—like studying for a final—and just listen to music, talk to a friend, draw, write, or walk the dog?

❏ While alcohol, tobacco, and drugs may seem to provide relief, am I willing to acknowledge that they actually increase stress levels and don't relieve the problem on a long-term basis?

❏ Do I beat myself up when I make a mistake? Do I have negative thoughts about myself and the direction my life is taking? Continually berating yourself increases the stress level.

❏ Am I a perfectionist? It's healthier to feel good about a "good enough" job.

❏ If I can't solve the big problems now, can I at least do something about the little ones?

❏ Stress causes fatigue and depression. Do I give myself time to get over them?

❏ Do I believe enough in myself and in my ability to take charge of my own life?

Signs That You May Need to Seek Help

❏ Withdrawing from friends and family, or alienating them

❏ Being sad, feeling empty or irritable almost all the time

❏ Finding little or no joy or pleasure in activities you've always enjoyed

❏ Blaming others

❏ Being unable to concentrate

❏ Having trouble sleeping, or sleeping all the time

❏ Always feeling guilty, helpless, or just plain worthless

❏ Having a significant weight loss or gain

❏ Feeling fatigued all the time

❏ Having recurring thoughts of death or suicide

Do not ignore the warning signs. If down moods persist for two weeks or more, seek professional help. You may be experiencing depression; effective treatments are available.

Resources to Tap

❏ Talk to a trusted adult, one who will respect your confidentiality.

❏ Visit with your school guidance counselor. If the counselor can't provide sufficient assistance, you may be referred to an outside professional.

❏ You can also be referred to a professional by a friend, your family doctor, a religious advisor, your local hospital or mental health center.

❏ Professionals include social workers, counselors, psychologists, and psychiatrists.

❏ Crisis hotlines allow you to call anonymously for information and advice.

❏ Contact the National Mental Health Association at www.nmha.org or 1-800-969-NMHA; or the National Alliance for the Mentally Ill at www.nami.org or 1-800-950-NAMI.

How Good Time Management Helps Balance a Potentially Stressful Load at School

My first three years [in high school], I carried full schedules with one study hall every other day. Senior year, I took 5.5 classes for credit—including three AP courses—and an ELP (Extended Learning Program) class worth half a credit. I never had many activities at the beginning of the school year, so I could get used to the class load. By December, I got hit and was busy the rest of the year. Still, my four or five serious activities didn't overlap, so except during tennis season, I didn't have something every night.

Our school gave us planners but I always forgot to write in mine. Then, my folks gave me a Palm Pilot, but I couldn't remember to write in it after every class either. I ended up selling it on eBay for more than it was worth.

What worked was an expandable file of clear plastic subject folders. I'd go through the folders at night and get all my homework done in one or two hours. Losing that folder would have been like wearing no pants to school. Plus, my mom kept track of my activities—tennis practice and matches and doctor's appointments—on a big kitchen calendar. If your parent is willing to do that, take advantage.

I also learned to utilize little bunches of time. Like nobody does anything until after dinner on Fridays, so I got in several hours of homework after school. I took homework to tennis meets. Once you've watched one tennis meet, you've watched them all. It amazes me what I could do in 20 minutes.

Ashlee Minton, Creighton University, Omaha, Nebraska

End-of-Chapter Questions

6.1 What exactly is stress, anyway?

6.2 What are some physical, emotional, and cognitive signs of stress?

6.3 What's an example of positive stress? Negative stress?

6.4 What are some of the causes of stress that I see in my own life?

6.5 What are some of the ways I can relieve stress?

6.6 When should I think about seeking outside help to handle the stress in my life? Where can I go for outside help?

Part 2
The College Search Is On

7

College Information—It's Everywhere!

In a world of uncertainty about college choices, this much is certain: you will receive a LOT of information about a LOT of colleges. The information will come from Internet searches, your high school counseling office, college admissions offices, little pieces of paper you filled out at college fairs, camps you attended, on-campus experiences in which you participated, good-to-great test scores you achieved, attention garnered for your ability as, perhaps, an athlete or a musician, and maybe a telemarketing list or two. You'll hear from colleges close to home, schools you've contacted, schools you've thought about, and schools you've never heard of.

In the beginning, all this attention is pretty exciting. But as the piles of materials grow, you may start feeling overwhelmed by how much information these colleges think you need. You can't read everything, but you don't want to toss anything that may be valuable as you move further into the selection process. If you limit your search only to schools you know about, you risk cutting yourself off from new experiences and opportunities down the road.

You'll learn, for example, that all colleges did not emerge from the same mold. In fact, some are truly unique. Simon's Rock College of Bard in Great Barrington, Massachusetts, is the nation's only four-year residential college of the liberal arts and sciences designed exclusively for students who have completed the 10th or 11th grade. They may earn an associate of arts degree in two years or a bachelor of arts degree after four years, and graduate two years ahead of their peers. Students at Reed College in Portland, Oregon, must take P.E. as well as read Herodotus and Virgil. On campus, students help staff a nuclear research reactor; off campus, they participate in mentor programs with local schools. Each student at War-

Know the College Semester Jargon

Semester plan: A fall semester, usually late August to mid-December, and a spring semester, usually mid-January to early May. The majority of institutions follow this plan, with individual variations. Students can expect to take five courses or about 15 credit hours per semester to graduate in four years.

4-1-4 plan: A fall and spring semester with a January term for focus on one course that encourages independent inquiry, innovation, or exploration of an area outside the student's usual purview. Earlham College in Richmond, Indiana, and Hawaii Pacific University in Honolulu follow this calendar.

Trimester plan: A fall semester, usually September to mid-December; a winter semester, usually January to mid-March; and a spring semester, usually late March to mid-June. Northwestern University in Evanston, Illinois, is one school that follows this plan.

12-12-6 plan: Three terms consisting of two 12-week semesters—called fall and winter terms—and one 6-week term—called spring term. Students take 12 to 14 credits during the longer terms and 3 to 6 credits in the spring term. At Washington and Lee University in Lexington, Virginia, the spring term consists of internships, brief study-abroad opportunities, fieldwork in the sciences, or focused foreign language conversations.

Winter study: Usually the month of January, this is an on- or off-campus class in an unusual topic or skill for credit or no credit.

One-course-at-a-time, also called the block plan: One course studied in-depth for 3½ weeks, with a few days' break in between each course. Generally, the class runs from 9 a.m. to noon, leaving afternoons for labs, studying, or researching. Students take eight or nine blocks from September to May, resulting in the same number of courses as students on the traditional semester system. Three U.S. colleges offer this plan: Cornell College, Mount Vernon, Iowa; Colorado College, Colorado Springs; and Tusculum College in Greenville, Tennessee.

ren Wilson College in Asheville, North Carolina, volunteers 100 hours to community service, receives room and board credit for a campus job, and carries a regular curricular load.

In the end, your first choice may be a school you had never heard of in the beginning. That means slowly sifting through computer printouts, glossy brochures, generic and personal letters. The real issue isn't whether you have enough information so much as whether you have the right information to reach your goal. And what is that goal? Finding a great match, which happens when College ABC is right for you and you are right for College ABC.

The Internet: A Great Place to Start

If you have particular schools in mind, visit their Web sites for information—videos, campus tours, admissions requirements, applications, tuition, financial aid, courses, majors, student and professor e-mail addresses, tips for incoming students, institutional history, a campus map . . . whatever you want to know. Use the school's e-mail address or phone number to request information via USPS or electronically.

Entering the key words "college search" in Google (www.google.com) yields a potpourri of choices—about 45 million within seconds! In fact, key words such as "college scholarships," "college admissions," or "college athletics" each yield several million sites to visit. Unless you have a ridiculous amount of time, you won't be able to visit several million sites. However, Google sites should be listed in order of relevance; the top sites are the ones used most by people like you. Google also has sponsored links that appear in a column along the right side of the page.

In addition, there are plenty of Web sites not connected with promoting any particular college. Rather, they contain a mother lode of information about thousands of colleges. For example, the *U.S. News & World Report*

How Can I Best Prepare for the College Search?

1. Am I open-minded about different possibilities as I start my college search? If not, why?

2. What is most important to me as I begin to create my own college ranking system?

3. Am I willing to put in the search time to make sure that where I end up is the best place for me?

4. How much time should I commit to surfing the Web for information?

5. Do I clearly understand how my high school counselor can help with this phase of the process?

How to Compare Colleges

At www.collegeboard.com, click on "College QuickFinder"; click "side-by-side comparison." At numeral 1, type in a college name; click "Go"; or select a college from the alphabetical lists. Click "Add" to include a college in your compare list, shown in numeral 2. Repeat the process to add colleges to the compare list. When you have two or three colleges on your compare list, click "Compare" at numeral 3. An easy-to-read chart compares the schools by location, type, campus, and student life (rural/urban setting and enrollment); admissions stats for percentage accepted, GPA of first-year students, application requirements (tests, interview), test scores of middle 50 percent of first-year students; cost and financial aid.

The same site's LikeFinder option performs a backward search to find schools similar to a college you know fits your size and cost parameters. From the home page click "College Search"; at LikeFinder, type your college preference/Go; on the new screen, click "LikeFind" under the college's name.

site (www.usnews.com/usnews/edu/college/corank.htm) ranks colleges in multiple categories such as Best Undergraduate Business Programs, Best Values: Great Schools at Great Prices, and Comprehensive Colleges—North (or South, West, or Midwest). Other sites may not rank, but do allow you to search by specifics such as name, major, state or region, cost, student life, and more.

You'll be introduced to admissions officers, students, and faculty and take a virtual tour of campuses. You can pull up very specific listings: historically black colleges, all-women's or all-men's colleges, Jesuit schools or Baptist colleges—even party schools! You can click your way through a process that matches your interests, areas of study, financial situation, and regional preferences with a corresponding list of colleges. The goal is to help you come up with the best combination of academics, environment, and affordability for you.

Your Personal Profile

Interactive Web sites invite you to complete a basic profile of your preferences, including region, estimated annual cost, freshman class size, surrounding community, and school type. Your responses can range from "doesn't matter" or "no preference" to being fairly specific—for example, you want to be part of a freshman class of fewer than 1,000. In return, you either receive a college list that matches your profile or you are informed

What You Need to Know about Filling Out Your Online Profile

❏ If you can't find a specific major listed in the areas of study, broaden your search. For example, if you want to major in biophysics but no colleges in your profile response offer it, select schools with a strong physics major program. Then visit those college sites listed in your search results, asking what they offer in biophysics.

❏ If you don't have a clue what your major may be—or how big or small a school should be, or whether you want to study in a small town or a big city, for example—leave related fields blank.

❏ Some highly selective schools have a need-blind policy, which means qualified students won't be denied admission because of financial need; the schools are prepared to offer full or partial scholarships and grants for demonstrated need. If you fit into that category, fill in the tuition field accordingly so as not to restrict your search.

❏ Search results are limited to colleges that generally accept students with scores from 20 percent below to 5 percent above your combined math-verbal SAT score. If you're at the top in your class, you may get a short list of possible schools. Try lowering the SAT scores you enter or leave them blank to get a more expansive list.

❏ It's the same with ACT scores. Colleges that require ACT scores less than three points below or two points above the score you entered won't show up on your list of schools.

there are no matches. In the latter case, change at least one of your responses and try again.

Some profiles are more detailed, asking for your preference as far as area of study, public/private, religious affiliation, ethnicity, special services, location, city size, student body type, athletics, and disabilities. You may also be asked for personal information such as test scores.

Try more than one site to see differences in the lists you get. Some major college search sites with profiling options include: the Princeton Review site (www.princetonreview.com) indicates your percent of fit with specific colleges based on your information and preferences. The College Board site (www.collegeboard.com) offers four search options: answer questions about your preferences and find schools that match, look at profiles of individual colleges, find colleges that match ones you're already interested in, and compare up to three schools side by side. *CollegesWantYou*, a feature on the Web site for Peterson's, part of the Thomson Corp. (www. petersons.com), allows you to have your completed profile sent to colleges that meet your specifications. The schools may contact you, but if they don't come knocking on your door, it's okay to contact them.

Counseling/Guidance Office: An Information Gold Mine

Your counselor plays a valuable role helping you navigate all those Web sites and sift through the resulting mountain of facts and figures for what you need to know. Plus, the counseling/guidance office has readily available information about in-state schools, the private schools within your state, and your community college system. Hopefully, the office also has drawer files chock-full of information about out-of-state colleges throughout the country—or, at the very least, the out-of-state colleges that attract your high school's graduates. Additionally, your counselor knows about college fairs in your area and visits by admissions representatives to your

Questions for My Counselor

- ❑ What Internet sites will be most helpful?
- ❑ Which of the big college guide books in the counseling office will be most helpful?
- ❑ What can I expect to get out of a college fair? Should I attend more than one?
- ❑ Can you put me in touch with our school's recent grads who attend colleges that might interest me?
- ❑ How does my high school compare to others in terms of test scores, AP courses, and overall reputation?
- ❑ Do you often work with students who want to attend highly selective schools? (If you're considering such schools but your counselor has little experience in that area, you may want to work with another counselor or a private independent counselor.)

school. Finally, unless your counselor is brand new to the job, he or she has been down this search road often. Don't underestimate the value of such hands-on experience.

While your counselor is there to help guide you through the college-search process, he or she may be responsible for guiding 400 (or more) other students as well. So make good use of your counselor's classroom presentations, handouts, parent/student meetings, and preplanned one-on-one sessions. If you need additional assistance or have questions, however, ask your counselor for help. Unanswered questions now could mean overlooked schools later.

The Private Independent Counselor

About 8 percent of students use private independent counselors in their college search. While the reasons vary, the fact is, a private counselor generally has more time to help with your college search. The flip side is that you—okay, your parents—pay for that help. Fees can start at about $400 and go up quickly, depending on which services you need for the application process.

In the past, independent counselors usually worked with students considering highly selective schools. Today they also have clients looking at state schools nationwide, rather than only in their home state. A counselor should not pick out the college for you; instead, the counselor should help you and your parents learn to assess what's important as you go through the search process.

If you decide to hire an independent counselor, check on professional affiliations, years in business, and where most clients have gone to college. Talk to the references listed. And watch out for people who want a cut of any aid you receive.

You've Got Mail! (In the Mailbox)

Typically, your first contact with a college will be a visit to its Web site; your second will be correspondence or a chat with the admissions officer—the most common entry point for interested high schoolers. Via a toll-free number or e-mail, you can ask the admissions officer to add your name to the school's database so you begin receiving printed and electronic materials. Often, one stream of information goes to high school sophomores or younger, another to juniors, and still another to seniors.

Six Ways to Organize All That Stuff

1. Keep information you receive in folders labeled "Very Appealing" schools, "Sounds Good Right Now" schools, "Okay" schools, and "I Don't Think So" schools.

2. Move Web site information and e-mails to similarly labeled files on your computer.

3. Add schools of interest to your favorite Web sites list.

4. As the folders grow (and they will), create a second set of folders and corresponding computer files. These will be for schools that are becoming increasingly interesting to you. Keep all information from School A in one folder or file, School B in a second folder or file, and so on.

5. You can set aside your "I Don't Think So" schools, and maybe even your "Okay" schools, but DON'T THROW ANYTHING AWAY YET! As you learn more about individual colleges and your own needs and wants, you may change your mind about your priorities. Sometimes, an "I Don't Think So" school becomes a "Sounds Good Right Now" school or even a "Very Appealing" school.

6. If all that organization is just too much for you, we did hear of one student who piled all the college brochures and papers into three super-size, green trash bags.

The younger you are, the more general the information. By the time you're a senior, information may relate to your area of academic interest as well as on-campus sports or activities in which you might want to participate.

The admissions officer also answers your e-mail or telephone questions and connects you with a particular coach, professor, program director, or current students. Generally, admissions officers are assigned to cover a geographic area so they get to know the schools in that area and become acquainted with prospective applicants through multiple contacts. Having someone in the admissions office who knows you can work to your advantage. Your goal right now, though, is to learn as much as you can about every college you're considering, so read that mail.

How I Organized My College Search

My family in general is organized—all the time. My mom was very supportive and had me thinking about and looking at colleges in junior high school. I had folders in our home office for each college, standardized tests, visits, and applications. There were still times we had to search for something, despite our orderliness.

I took the SAT and ACT multiple times starting in junior high, so I received lots of information from colleges. But it can get overwhelming if you have too much information and no system. If you have just garbage bags full of information, take a weekend, go through it, and try to get it down to fewer colleges. Don't keep information from other state schools if you know you only want to go to one school in your state.

We organized college visits to go to more than one school per trip. The exception was Pittsburgh because there were no other schools close that I was interested in. A big incentive to come to Pittsburgh was the money they offered me, but I wanted to see it and not base my decision solely on the money.

By the time March and April of my senior year rolled around, I knew all the vital information about the schools I'd applied to. There are so many variables to keep straight, so I made a chart of my top three schools to compare the important things about each and why I would want to go here or there. College is an important decision and a big investment, so you must be organized to figure out what is best for you.

Stephanie Smith, University of Pittsburgh, Pennsylvania

End-of-Chapter Questions

7.1 What kinds of college search information can I get on the Internet? How can I sort out which Web sites will be helpful to me?

7.2 When I find similar schools, do I run side-by-side comparisons for a more thorough understanding of each school's qualities?

7.3 What personal information should I include in my basic profile? What personal likes and dislikes should I consider?

7.4 Do I have a major (or two) in mind? If yes, what are they? If no, what topics sound appealing as I look over the vast array of possible majors?

7.5 If no major sounds appealing right now, what other factors should I research in this beginning phase of the college search process?

7.6 How frequently should I touch base with my counselor so that he or she knows me by name and by need? Do I consider how busy my counselor may be with all those other students? Should I make appointments ahead of time?

7.7 How do I utilize all the information from my counselor?

7.8 How can I best use those big college books?

7.9 Can my parents come to the counseling office when they need information? How faithful are my parents and I about attending counselor sessions geared toward families?

7.10 When I learn about college fairs in my area, do I mark them down on the calendar? Should I attend them with or without my parents?

7.11 How can I treat every contact with a new admissions counselor as the beginning of a potentially long-term relationship? What is the college admissions officer's or dean's role in my search process? How does my high school counselor view his or her role in advocating for me with the admissions office?

7.12 What organizational system will best help me sort out the information I know I need, the information I may need, and the information I probably will never need?

8

All Kinds of Colleges

Choosing where to go to college is like trying to choose just one of Ben and Jerry's ice cream flavors on a hot day. Chocolate Chip Cookie Dough ice cream appeals one time but Cherry Garcia ice cream sounds better another. Colleges will attract you in varying degrees too, as you go through the search and application process.

After all, there are literally thousands of accredited colleges and universities in this country: more than 2,300 four-year schools and more than 1,800 two-year schools. One of the smallest, Sierra Nevada College–Lake Tahoe in Incline Village, Nevada, has fewer than 350 undergraduates. One of the largest, the University of Texas at Austin, has about 39,000 full- and part-time undergraduate students. Big, small, and all the sizes in between—each has advantages and disadvantages. And you get to choose which ones matter to you and your family.

What Kind of School Fits Me Best?

If each person in your family began his or her postsecondary education at your local community college, then finished up at State U, should you follow in those footsteps? If everyone as far back as your great-grandparents studied at the same small school in Southern California, should you forget your dream of going to a big school in Michigan?

Not necessarily.

Schools are like shoes: one size doesn't fit all. Figuring out what appeals to you and what is distasteful, what's comfortable and what pinches—basically, what you like and don't like—is the first step in deciding where to apply. Let's face it, if you absolutely hate snow, Colorado may not be the place for you, no matter how many friends say it's their number one choice.

To figure out which schools suit you, begin by considering four basic options: state, private, highly selective colleges and universities, and community colleges. Included in that mix are four-year liberal arts colleges, both private and state. Liberal arts colleges offer bachelor's degrees, are generally smaller than universities, have smaller classes taught by professors, and focus on graduating students in four years. Universities, both private and state, offer bachelor's, master's, and, usually, doctorate degrees. Universities are composed of a liberal arts college, professional colleges, and graduate programs. They generally have larger freshman classes that are often taught in lecture format by graduate assistants. Students must plan carefully to be able to complete studies in four years.

State Colleges and Universities

The big news with state colleges and universities is the changing student body. State-of-the-art teaching, combined with tuition price tags that are usually significantly lower than those at private institutions, are resulting in more highly qualified students applying. This is turning some state

Fast Facts about State Schools

- ❑ There are approximately 640 state colleges and universities in this country.
- ❑ Total enrollment is about 6.3 million students.
- ❑ More than 8 in 10 schools do not have an open admissions policy, so applicants must meet standards, which vary from one school to another.
- ❑ Some schools consider only objective data for admissions, which may include GPA, class rank, and the SAT or ACT score.
- ❑ Others consider multiple criteria—activities, recommendations, and sometimes an essay—in addition to objective scores and grades.
- ❑ Although some schools use computer databases to sort applications, the admissions staff reviews applications for admit or deny decisions.
- ❑ Tuition and fees average almost $4,700 per year for state residents and $11,750 for out-of-state residents.

Why I Chose a State School

Taking entrance exams gave me a realistic idea of where I could be admitted. I applied to the University of Minnesota because my test scores guaranteed admission. I also applied to two liberal arts schools—Carleton and Northwestern. Lots of kids in my high school Honors programs applied to Carleton; I knew my scores were the mean for freshmen. And I applied to Princeton and Harvard. I wanted to get into the best school I could, but had to make sure I got into some school.

I got into Carleton and was wait-listed at Northwestern, but chose the U of M. Private schools don't offer as many degree programs as public universities, which enabled me to be more open-minded in my degree decision. Colleges within the U of M have Honors programs. So I applied to the Institute of Technology and got into that college's Honors program. Those were separate procedures, just like applying to a select university because of what you had to do to get in. Also, a liberal arts school costs $30,000 a year, and I'm paying about $8,000. The U is fairly close to where I live, so I commute and save money. And there are more research opportunities because the U of M gets federal and state funds that private schools don't. Its chemical engineering program is ranked number one in the nation. I took all those factors into consideration.

Goher Mahmoud, University of Minnesota, Minneapolis

schools—particularly big research schools, which are in almost every state—into highly competitive admissions clubs. Many schools have developed an Honors program within the university to challenge academic whiz kids. However, because state-funded schools were created to offer a postsecondary educational opportunity to as many as possible, these schools also offer remedial classes. In fact, more students are enrolling in remedial courses at the beginning of their college career.

Another issue is tight budgets. Many states are cutting funds to their state institutions. The impact is being felt by students through increasing tuition and fees, larger classes, and fewer class choices, all of which affect you as a prospective student.

Private Colleges and Universities

Private schools vary widely in size, location, academic programs, and institutional missions. For instance:

❏ Brigham Young University in Provo, Utah, with more than 26,000 students, is affiliated with the Church of Jesus Christ of Latter-day Saints.

❏ Landmark College in Putney, Vermont, is a two-year school with about 400 students, exclusively serving students with dyslexia, AD/HD (attention deficit hyperactivity disorder), or specific learning disabilities.

❏ Wilmington College in New Castle, Delaware, is nonresidential, open access, and nonsectarian, with more than 7,500 students.

Admissions standards generally vary from open access to highly selective. The schools are financed by tuition, fees, and endowment earnings; gifts from individuals, businesses, and foundations; and some government appropriations.

Fast Facts about Private Schools

❏ There are about 1,600 private two- and four-year colleges and universities in the United States.

❏ Tuition and fees average $19,710.

❏ The average tuition that students pay at private colleges has actually declined over the past decade, once you subtract grant aid and adjust for inflation.

❏ Two-thirds of grants given consider financial need; one-third is based entirely on factors other than need.

❏ The proportion of students from racial and ethnic minorities is almost the same as at four-year state schools.

❏ Students who work full-time, have a high school equivalency diploma, or face other challenges are more likely to graduate from a private school than from a state school.

❏ Students are as likely to earn their degree in four years at a private school as they are in six years at a state school.

Why I Chose a Private School

I thought at first I would have to go to a public school, in-state, because I couldn't afford a private school. After applying to different places, I found that a private school can be cheaper.

At first I looked at smaller colleges fairly close to where I live [Harrogate, Tennessee].

Then, for the heck of it, I printed out the list of the top 200 liberal arts colleges from U.S. News, did a search on www.collegeboard.com for colleges that fit my criteria, and visited the Web sites of the schools that appeared on both lists. Once I got my list down to 10, I called admissions offices.

Through that search, I ended up here with a full scholarship. I was also offered a half scholarship from Centre College [Danville, Kentucky]. When I went there for the Governor's Scholars Program, I was with 300 students and got the feel of a small college. Actually, as a Governor's Scholar, I could have had my way paid at a state school. But at a private school you hardly ever have a class of more than 25, and for the majority of professors, teaching is their focus. They do research as well, but their main focus is students. I've been asked out to lunch by every one of my professors. That would not happen in a class with 200 kids. Here, if you need help, you have the professors' phone numbers.

I highly encourage anyone interested in a private college to let people in the admissions office know you really want to attend that school. Call and let them know how things are going.

**Brandon Carmack, Hobart and William Smith Colleges,
Geneva, New York**

Highly Selective Colleges and Universities

Unlike state schools, private schools, and community colleges, there is no standard definition for a highly selective school. Still, about 30 private colleges and universities, along with a few public institutions, such as University of Michigan, University of Pennsylvania, and University of Virginia, are considered highly selective.

These highly selective schools are, quite frankly, really tough to get into. Some have traditionally had very high admissions standards; others have,

Fast Facts about Highly Selective Schools

❏ Highly selective schools receive far more applications than they can possibly accept. For example, Princeton (New Jersey) University receives more than 14,000 applications, admits about 2,700, and actually enrolls about 1,200 in a freshman class.

❏ Really high or even perfect SAT/ACT scores do not guarantee admission.

❏ Applications are more involved, requiring one or more essays.

❏ Applicants compete through above-average grades in tough courses (Honors, AP), stratospheric test scores, GPA, class rank, teacher recommendations, extracurricular activities, community service, and demonstration of leadership.

❏ All applications are read, often more than once, sometimes by people outside as well as inside the admissions office.

of late, become much more selective. In fact, compared to 1992, admissions standards for four-year private institutions were higher in the year 2000—higher tests scores, higher GPA/class rank. Additionally, acceptance rates were lower. The bottom line? More highly qualified applicants are competing for limited space in highly selective private schools.

Admissions officers wade through pools of applicants, plucking out the best of the best. But this is no random plucking. They're attempting to sculpt well-rounded classes, bringing together students who will learn from one another. They want athletes and musicians and thinkers and artists and leaders. And they get very specific. As one private admissions consultant said, "If Harvard is losing a tuba player, then Harvard is conscious of that." These schools consider just about everything, right down to geography. If you live in an area that tends not to send lots of students to highly selective schools, you may stand a better chance of admittance than students in a private, prep high school—but only if your test scores are way up there. So check criteria for admission in those big books in your school's counseling office, study the profiles of typical entering students, and be sure to apply to a couple safety schools where you are positive of being accepted.

There are benefits to being one of the chosen few. You're among students who, for downtime, talk about Chaucer or Jung or AIDS in Africa. You may make contacts that lead to professions such as investment banking, where starting salaries are close to six figures. You receive instant re-

Why I Chose a Highly Selective School

I went to Loyola High School in Los Angeles, a private, all-male, Jesuit institution. It's actually very hard to get into so I've been in a competitive environment since before I can remember. If I had not gone there, I wouldn't even know what Brown is. I began taking a lot of Honors classes when I was a freshman. I hadn't planned to, but all these kids were taking such hard classes that I didn't want to be behind. Sophomore year, we took an East Coast college tour and I first saw Brown. I applied early decision to Georgetown, and when I didn't get in, I applied to other schools, and Brown, but at the last minute. I almost didn't complete my application because I didn't think I could get in.

I like that there's no core curriculum; it's a liberal school. It's a lot more work. First semester, I had no sit-in exams, but rather take-home final papers for four classes. I ended up writing 50 pages. I was very thankful my high school prepared us.

Being here has already opened doors. Last summer I got two multicultural internships at the Getty [Center] in L.A. I didn't realize how much of an impact Brown would have. I was going through interviews and people were very impressed.

Brown has a need-blind admission policy, so it doesn't look at an applicant's family income. That allows for a diverse array of kids from different economic backgrounds. I work in Brown's admissions office in minority recruitment, including inner-city L.A. schools because most of those kids don't get the opportunity to know about schools like this. I tell them you don't know if you can get in until you give it a shot. Tons of kids who apply are straight-A students with good SAT scores, but that's it. Brown is looking for all-around students who are academically smart but also active in their communities or school activities, athletics, and programs.

Paul Aguliar, Brown University, Providence, Rhode Island

spect for applications to postgraduate degree programs—and bragging rights for you and your parents, which is important to some.

Community Colleges

These can be public community colleges (also called junior and technical colleges), public and private centers, or institutes and specialty schools for art, music, aviation, and other disciplines. They offer two-year associate

Fast Facts about Community Colleges

- ❏ Our 1,100 community colleges have a combined enrollment of 5.6 million students. They represent 45 percent of all undergraduates.
- ❏ Tuition and fees average $1,904.
- ❏ 55 percent of all first-year college students begin at a community college.
- ❏ Tuition and fees at a community college average approximately half of those at public, four-year colleges; they are less than 15 percent of what private, four-year schools charge.
- ❏ As many students enroll half-time as full-time because they work. Consequently, community colleges offer classes and programs at times and places convenient for working students, including nights and weekends.
- ❏ Community college students tend to live off campus, often at home to save money. Some campuses have no dormitories.

degrees, diploma programs, and certificates, which are issued upon completion of classes in a specialty area, such as welding.

Community colleges traditionally have maintained an open-door policy, meaning admission has been automatic with proof of a high school diploma or equivalent. But that's changing. Many community colleges are raising their admission standards and academic curriculum, and first-year students tend to do as well academically as freshmen at four-year schools.

Most community colleges now provide course requirements for students moving into four-year schools, including highly competitive public universities. These requirements, incorporated into articulation agreements between schools, comply with programs—such as a nursing program—and curricular offerings at those four-year schools. The Illinois Articulation Initiative, for example, considers any graduate with a degree from an accredited Illinois community college to have satisfied all the general education requirements at certain four-year public colleges and universities in the state.

If you're thinking about a community college, ask what courses transfer, how easy it is to transfer, and how well the transfer students do compared with students already at the four-year schools you're considering. Additionally, check your state or neighboring states for articulation agreements between community and four-year state colleges.

Why I Chose a Community College

When I was a senior, I looked at four-year colleges and this community college and thought they were pretty similar except that some of the four-year schools were pretty big. I was a little scared of getting lost in that size school so I thought the community college would be a better fit to start with.

This school also is a lot cheaper, and I'm getting the same general education that anyone would get at a four-year college. The biggest benefits for me are the smaller classes and the personal attention you receive from professors. My biggest class has about 25 students. I have some very caring professors who really do pay attention to their students. My math professor recommended I go to the tutoring center, and that's really helped.

Some friends looked down on me for going to a community college, but I tell them it's not any easier than a four-year university. I have met people such as an anesthetist who started at a community college, so I know I will be able to jump-start from here to a career path I want. I'll get an associate of arts degree and the credits will transfer to any state school and most private schools in Minnesota.

I live in one of two dorm complexes about five minutes from school. We have a kitchen, living room, four private bedrooms, and two private baths. I'm actually in the dorm that's a little more of a party dorm, but I usually just put on classical music with my headphones so I can study. People pretty much go home every weekend, and so do I. It's about an hour's drive.

I'm glad I came here and would suggest people don't rule out going to a community college just because you think people will look down on you. It is a viable option.

Danielle Hensley, Minnesota State Community and Technical College, Fergus Falls

End-of-Chapter Questions

8.1 What are my priorities right now as far as what I want from a college?

8.2 Should I choose a college just because my parent or other relative graduated from there? How much influence should my friends have on my choice?

8.3 What is the difference between a state and private institution? What are the differences in terms of curriculum and class size? Why should I think about these differences?

8.4 Are professors equally accessible in state and private schools?

8.5 Why should I think about the campus environment? What does a state school offer in terms of environment compared to a private school?

8.6 What is a liberal arts college? What is the difference between a college and a university?

8.7 Am I aware of costs at any state and private schools I'm interested in?

8.8 Do my classes, GPA, test scores, extracurricular activities, and community service commitments fall within the profile range of state schools? Private schools? Highly selective schools?

8.9 Do I understand how competitive admissions are at highly selective schools? Do I still think I am a sure bet to get in if I apply to 15 highly selective schools?

8.10 Do I have information on small, medium, and large four-year colleges, as well as community colleges?

8.11 What kinds of degrees do community colleges grant? Why would I consider going to a community college if I want a bachelor's degree?

8.12 If I am considering a community college as a step toward transferring to a four-year school, have I checked the community college's accreditation? Will my class credits transfer to the four-year schools in which I'm interested? Is English 101 academically equal to English 101 at the four-year college I might transfer to?

8.13 Do I know if the community college has a steady number of students transferring to any particular four-year school?

9

Parameters for Choosing Colleges

Which parameters should I consider when choosing a college? "All of them!" That's the short and easy answer. Warning: One college won't offer everything you like. But it should offer everything you need. Ultimately, you'll need to choose which parameters are more important than others.

Don't make those decisions right now, though. One academic whiz kid we know immediately tossed out any college that had more females than males. After she graduated from college, she said, "You know, I probably should have looked at women's colleges when I was deciding. I would have liked that environment better."

What Are Your Priorities?

The college you select will be "home" for the next four *big* years of your life. New people, new ideas, new teachers, new friends, new books, new jobs, new . . . Well, you get the idea. All that change doesn't have to be totally surprising *if you do your homework on selecting the right school for you.* You'll need to consider and chart your priorities for environment, academics, and costs and look at each college to see how it fits you.

What Do I Like and Dislike?

What I like about my high school:	What I don't like about my high school:
1. _____	1. _____
2. _____	2. _____
3. _____	3. _____

What I like about my community:	What I don't like about my community:
1. _____	1. _____
2. _____	2. _____
3. _____	3. _____

What I like about living at home:	What I don't like about living at home:
1. _____	1. _____
2. _____	2. _____
3. _____	3. _____

Aspects to Consider

You should consider the following 16 parameters when determining which colleges fit your needs and wants.

School Size

Students at small schools have the opportunity to become better acquainted with their instructors, professors, and classmates. This is especially true during the first year, when some lecture classes at many large schools contain hundreds of students and may be taught by graduate students rather than professors. On the other hand, larger schools generally offer more areas of study. Another difference is that the larger the school, the more extracurricular activities and intramural offerings there are to choose from. But then, the smaller the school, the more opportunity there is to participate in the activities and offerings.

Big or Small: Which Sounds Better to Me?

❑ If you are in a small high school, what attracts you about attending a large college? And if you are in a large high school, what's attractive about a small college?

❑ Do I usually thrive on change or suffer through it?

Going from a Large High School to a Small College

My high school has 2,200 students and about 450 in my graduating class. [Harvey Mudd has 680.] I wanted a good college; size was secondary. I considered Harvard, Stanford, UCLA, Berkeley, and Harvey Mudd and was accepted at UCLA, Berkeley, and Harvey Mudd.

I'd taken classes at UCLA and everything was anonymous, which I like. But my mom is going for her second Ph.D. at UCLA and I didn't want to go there because of that. She was a teacher at my high school as well, so I'd had enough of that. I visited Berkeley because I actually wanted a bigger school, but it was physically dirty and people were, in general, too liberal for my taste.

Harvey Mudd was stressful at first. They have student mug shots so all the professors know who you are before you even go to class. I was used to not having anyone know who I was, and I liked it that way. I always liked to have my own group of friends and kept a certain degree of separation from people I wouldn't normally associate with.

A small school helped me become more accepting. Growing up in L.A. puts you in a superficial environment, but that's not the case at a small college. Here, you know everyone simply by being in the same environment. Now, I like people I normally wouldn't associate with—just by getting to know them, talking to them, and finding commonalities. I saw intellectual similarities and have come to appreciate and even like other students who, in high school, I would have considered social undesirables.

Steve Lin, Harvey Mudd College, Claremont, California

Geography

Columbia University is in New York City, home to more than 8 million residents. Grinnell College is in Grinnell, Iowa, home to about 9,000 residents. Like school size, locations have advantages and disadvantages. You could probably go to a different movie theater every night of the school year in New York City and still not hit them all. In Grinnell, there's one theater, but you can bike around town or even out in the countryside when you're sick of studying. Again, don't automatically rule out any location at this point.

Big City School? Small Town School?

If you're from a small town or rural area, name three advantages of choosing a college in a city.	If you're from a city, name three advantages of choosing a college in a small town or rural area.
1. _____	1. _____
2. _____	2. _____
3. _____	3. _____
What three favorite things do I like about where I live now?	What three things do I dislike about where I live now?
1. _____	1. _____
2. _____	2. _____
3. _____	3. _____

More Geography: Searching for a Different Way of Life

Ever wonder what the rest of the world is like? Going to school in a different part of the country can yield not only a college degree but also a new perspective on life in general. If you grew up in Montana, for example, you'll find life at the University of Miami to be an education in itself. There's an ocean, for starters, and probably more pizza take-out places in the city than in the whole state of Montana. Same for the Miami student who heads out to Montana State University-Bozeman and finds no traffic jams and a view of seven mountain ranges from a nearby hiking trail.

How Independent Do I Want to Be?

Answer yes or no:
1. If the campus is just a neighborhood away from home, will I feel as though I'm still tethered to the family and community life? _____
2. Will I learn to do my own laundry? _____
3. Will I learn to cope with homesickness? _____
4. If I can't spend Thanksgiving with my family because of the distance away from home, will I—and they—mind? _____

Going Away Close to Home

For me, it's a shorter distance to Georgetown than to my high school, also in Washington. Georgetown draws people from all over the country and the world, and I have one of the shortest trips. I can move in and out easily. I can basically drive up and drop stuff off—25 minutes to get down there. And if I forget anything, I can go back and get it. I did take more stuff that would have been harder to take on a plane. I had a desktop computer rather than a laptop.

My first semester I went home a great deal because I had things I was trying to do. I was able to become an Eagle Scout and complete a requirement for my driver's education certification. If I hadn't lived nearby, I wouldn't have been able to do that. So I was coming home a great deal but only as long as I needed to finish something, and then I went back to Georgetown. I never did laundry at home.

I've not been forced to go home. And my parents have given me space—they don't show up on campus much. So even though I'm familiar with the city and Georgetown, it's a whole different experience. It's been the best possible situation for me. And in my junior year I will do a semester or a year study abroad to get away. I might even be interested in New Zealand, which is pretty far away.

Andrew Balkam, Georgetown University, Washington, D.C.

Cost

Tuition can range anywhere from about $3,100 a year at Missouri Southern State University in Joplin to more than $30,000 a year at Brown University in Providence, Rhode Island. Factor in also room and board, mandatory fees, books, transportation, and personal costs. College guides and Web sites list such costs, usually stating an average for items such as personal costs.

People automatically think it's cheaper to attend a state school than a private one. And it may be, if the state school is in the state in which you live. Florida State University in Tallahassee, for example, charges Floridians about $3,000 tuition and non-Floridians about $14,000. If you want to go to a state school outside your home state, find out from the school how to qualify as a resident in that other state before enrolling. However, no matter where your state-of-residence, you'll need to factor in whether you will need more than four years at a state school to complete your degree requirements.

Many private schools offer more financial aid to lessen and sometimes erase the gap between public and private schools. Your best bet is to not discount a school you think is beyond reach financially until you call the financial aid office at the school and discuss your situation.

Religious Affiliation

More than 650 schools are affiliated with a religion. Some, such as Texas Christian University in Fort Worth, have only nominal affiliation; others, like Marquette University in Milwaukee, Wisconsin, are run by the Society of Jesus, a Catholic religious order commonly referred to as the Jesuits.

 **What Part Does Religion Play
in My College Choice?**

❏ Is going to a religiously affiliated school important to me? To my parents?

❏ If my parents and I differ about attending a religiously affiliated school, what will it take for us to agree?

❏ Are there religiously affiliated schools offering areas of concentration or majors that interest me?

Choosing a Faith-Based School

When I was young, my parents were missionaries in India. We moved back when I was in eighth grade so I could go to high school in the States. I was in [public] high school choir and in Texas All-State Choir for three years. I'd been recruited by different schools in this state—Texas Tech, the University of Texas, Baylor—because I was going to major in vocal performance.

I visited some colleges, then talked to LCU. I knew I wanted to be here because religion is the main focus. Bible classes are required four semesters and you can take more. Everyone attends chapel every day. Your religious life comes before anything else. Through clubs and organizations, you get to know people who have the same thinking as you. And it's neat to see your professor all week at school, then go to church on Sunday morning and see your professor. Prayer is a big thing on campus. Community service is a big thing on campus. I can find a good Christian wife here with the same beliefs as me. I've made relationships here that will last forever with other Christian people. When I struggle with stuff here, other Christians can help me.

I had a free ride at a state university. My parents weren't too thrilled when I said I wanted to pass that up. LCU is really good at working with you on scholarships and stuff like that. I got different scholarships here and only pay about $1,000 a year.

LCU's music department is not up to the same standards as public universities yet, so I'm a secondary education major and I sing in one of the groups here. I know anywhere I go, I'll always be involved in music.

My parents in retrospect think it was the best decision. I chose to surround myself with people who have the same moral standards and thinking faithwise, and make a life for myself from that aspect. It all boils down to my being Christian as more important than pursuing a musical and acting career.

Josh Wheeler, Lubbock (Texas) Christian University

Coed versus Single Gender Schools

Half a century ago about 75 percent of colleges and universities in this country were coeducational. The remainder was split evenly between schools solely for men and solely for women. Today, of the remaining single gender schools, 68 schools accept only women and 15 accept only men.

Research suggests that only 3 percent of high school girls have a serious interest in attending an all-women's college. However, women's college graduates constitute more than 20 percent of women in Congress and 30 percent of a *BusinessWeek* list of rising women in business; yet these women represent only 2 percent of all female college graduates. Schools accepting only men are, mostly, seminaries or rabbinical colleges, although six are secular institutions: Morehouse College, Atlanta, Georgia; Wabash College, Crawfordsville, Indiana; Hampden-Sydney (Virginia) College; Deep Springs College, Inyo County, California; the undergraduate program at St. John's University, Collegeville, Minnesota; and Valley Forge Military College, Wayne, Pennsylvania.

 ## Choosing an All-Women's School and Liking It

I wasn't actually looking for an all-girls school, but Randolph-Macon sent me literature, and the academics and programs were comparable to what else I was looking at, so I was interested. In the end, I visited there and the U of Georgia, a very large school. I felt at home right away at Randy-Mac. I ride horses, and it offers an excellent equestrian program, which all-girls schools often have. Then, things started popping into mind: Would I ever see guys there? Are there strict rules and policies to follow? And there was always the lesbian issue, that all-girls schools are only for lesbians. That's a stereotype I had to consider.

None of my fears were true. I came from a coed high school, and my parents wanted me to go where I felt happy. I am from Fort Wayne, so I got a lot of, "Why didn't you just go to St. Mary's in South Bend?" Well, not all all-girls schools are the same.

It's a family environment here. Some nights, it's like a big slumber party. Professors know you and take your interests to heart. I realize some of this attention has to do with being such a small school, but I think if this were coed, it wouldn't be the same. All-girls schools make you independent, more assertive and free thinking.

Beth Anne Zielinski, Randolph-Macon Woman's College, Lynchburg, Virginia

What Part Does Gender Play in My College Choice?

❏ What's been my experience with a female- or male-only environment? If the answer is "none," how can I find someone to talk to who has attended a single gender high school or college?

❏ Are there single gender schools that offer areas of concentration or majors of interest to me?

❏ If I'm hesitant to consider a single gender school, can I pinpoint reasons why?

❏ Would I be happy without daily interaction with the opposite sex?

Military Academies

If the notion of a military academy appeals to you, spend some time at one of our five academies before signing on. They are: U.S. Air Force Academy, Colorado Springs, Colorado; U. S. Military Academy, West Point, New York; U.S. Naval Academy, Annapolis, Maryland; U.S. Merchant Marine Academy, Kings Point, New York; and the U.S. Coast Guard Academy, New London, Connecticut.

Just like visiting a college campus, you need to get the "feel" of both the place and the atmosphere. Seek out recent graduates as well as present students to assess their comfort level with school routines and policies. The application process at all but two of the academies differs significantly from those at nonmilitary schools and requires that you begin in your junior year at high school. Certainly, the price is right (free), although you do pay Uncle Sam back with service after graduation.

Student Body

Most college freshmen are three months out of high school and live in a residence hall on campus. Some colleges, however, attract more 20-something students who go to school part-time and live off campus. In that instance, if you're an 18-year-old in a residence hall, you might become lonely.

Ethnicity

No matter what your ethnicity, diversity will probably be part of your college experience. Most schools aim to admit students who don't look or act or think just like you. Some schools, though, have a stronger commitment to diversity than others.

What Part Does Ethnicity Play in My College Choice?

❑ Would I be more comfortable socially and intellectually at a school where a small percent of students share my ethnicity? Or would I rather go to a school where a large percentage share my ethnicity? Why?

❑ How would a campus with a mix of ethnic groups benefit me?

Choosing a Historically Black College

My hometown is about 30,000 and my high school was predominantly black. I wanted to attend an institution I could relate to, though I didn't see that as depending on the color of my fellow students. I wanted a college that would pull the inward me out, so I could be who I had the potential to be. We all have potential to be the better part of ourselves. We can all strive and grow to become better.

I wanted a college that was prestigious as well as accredited, a school that had a reputation of producing students who think like me. My first visit at Tougaloo College was for my cousin's graduation. As I walked into the gymnasium, I heard the sounds of African drums playing and I felt the heartbeat of Tougaloo College. I fell in love with the atmosphere and I knew this was the place for me. It was rhythmic, harmonious. That's what I was looking for. I needed an institution that would be one with me.

I didn't seek out an African American college, but I knew when I found Tougaloo, that's where I would go. It just so happened to be a historically black college.

I would advise young black students to visit historically black institutions because people like them will be going to those schools. I'm not saying white institutions can't provide what you need, but at least see what a historically black school has to offer.

Timothy Crear, Tougaloo (Mississippi) College

Graduation Rate

Some colleges graduate nearly all of their students. Others graduate significantly less. A lower graduation rate may raise some red flags about whether the school accepts students who are not qualified or the environment is not to students' liking. Ask about the graduation rate and why it's high or low. Also, ask how many students graduate in four years.

Freshman Living Arrangements

Where you live your freshman year can have a powerful impact on making a healthy adjustment to campus life. Know what's available—including how the school handles overcrowding when all those freshmen show up on campus. Believe it or not, some schools deal with overcrowding by herding freshmen into the gym for the first few weeks of school.

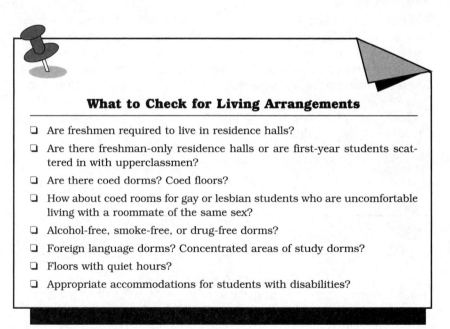

What to Check for Living Arrangements

- ❏ Are freshmen required to live in residence halls?
- ❏ Are there freshman-only residence halls or are first-year students scattered in with upperclassmen?
- ❏ Are there coed dorms? Coed floors?
- ❏ How about coed rooms for gay or lesbian students who are uncomfortable living with a roommate of the same sex?
- ❏ Alcohol-free, smoke-free, or drug-free dorms?
- ❏ Foreign language dorms? Concentrated areas of study dorms?
- ❏ Floors with quiet hours?
- ❏ Appropriate accommodations for students with disabilities?

Four-Year Living Arrangements

Where will you live after your freshman year? Does the college have enough housing guaranteed if you want to live on campus? Would the school require you to live in a residence hall if space is available rather than in the Greek house you've joined?

School Reputation

Every school seems to have a reputation. Studious. Party. Very Greek. Full of jocks. One way to determine whether that reputation is accurate may be from a campus visit where you schedule times to talk to students and faculty. Or talk with a recent graduate whom you know or students from your school who go there.

Campus Safety

Sure, you know nothing will ever happen to you, but check out items that your parents worry about anyway, such as transportation, night lighting, and the availability of phones to call security.

Internships

You can get wonderful hands-on experience—not to mention an inside track for a job after graduation—through internships. This experiential learning provides a real-world understanding of the workplace, its challenges and rewards. You should be able to practice communication skills, develop a network of relationships, and come to appreciate the importance of your academic world. Opportunities run the gamut—accounting, trucking, insurance, engineering, architecture, sports/recreation, law enforcement, public relations—and that's just for starters.

Internships That Work

❑ Does the college help students connect with internships in my area of interest during the summer? During the school year?

❑ What percent of students obtain internships? Do only top students get internships?

❑ Do interns get paid? Do they get class credit?

❑ Do companies tend to hire their interns after graduation?

Major

The ideal is to choose a college that offers a strong program in your major. For instance, if you are interested in theater, a college that puts on two

Switching Majors

I live with six girls and four have changed majors. It's not unusual.

I came to college thinking I'd be a premed major. But that first semester, I still wanted to try a lot of different things rather than be locked into premed. I talked to the department heads in biology and premed. You think when you're a freshman that they're so big and don't have time for you, but that's not so.

Although I didn't like every class I explored, I figured if someone teaches me something, it's my responsibility to learn it. At the same time, I didn't know if I would like it unless I attempted to learn it. Also, I've always taken around 17 credits each semester. I always felt like I'm paying for 18 credits so why take 12?

I tried an economics course and liked it. When I talked to the econ department head, he said to take a couple business courses, and I really liked the accounting. Most business majors hate it, but I was sitting in class and couldn't wait to go home and start my homework.

After sophomore year I decided to major in accounting and minor in economics. I can definitely graduate in four years, but because I am going to study abroad next semester, I will have to pick up two summer school classes between my junior and senior year and also take 18 credits every remaining semester.

The only setback I've had is not anticipating things that are supposed to happen in junior and senior year. For example, my accounting advisor said that as a junior, there's no way I can study abroad because of needing to do internships that year. We talked about it further, discussed my GPA, and found a way.

If you don't know what to major in, just keep an open mind. Take a lot of courses and follow your instincts. See what you really think you're doing well in or have some excitement for. Definitely plan, know your options, but don't overthink, because it works out.

Danielle Austin, Ithaca (New York) College

plays a year but offers neither a drama major nor related courses makes little sense, even if the campus is beautiful. The problem is, most high school students don't know what they want to major in. And if they do, most will change that major after sampling a variety of college classes. Still, certain areas of study may grab your attention, so look at colleges that offer related programs. Your major—and career opportunities—may well emerge from those classes.

Generally speaking, the larger the school, the more majors and areas of concentration offered. Even so, big schools, just like smaller ones, can be known for particular strengths.

10 Good Reasons to Choose a College

1. The academics include lots of great courses in your possible major or areas about which you are curious.

2. A high percentage of freshmen who start at the college graduate from there.

3. The workload appears to be academically challenging, but not out of your reach.

4. There are a variety of intramural or club sports teams to consider joining.

5. The extracurricular offerings align closely with your interests.

6. You and your parents feel comfortable about the distance from college to home.

7. The size of the student body is what you had in mind.

8. You've spent time thinking about what you like and don't like in a college and, as best as possible, have put aside notions about what is trendy.

9. You've spoken with graduates of the college, and they are happy with their educational experience.

10. The school emphasizes certain areas—ethnicity, gender, faith, community, academics, art, music, sports—that are important to you.

When the College You've Chosen Isn't the Right One for You

I hated high school. I was good in English, bad at math. But instead of working with my strengths in English to keep me challenged, I got put into regular track programs because of math scores. I had an abysmal 1.8 GPA, but high test scores and a strong extracurricular record. I got 34 on the ACT.

My senior year I participated in a bridge program—half-day high school, half-day college. Sort of got my feet wet with the university. I also got into a summer bridge program for the sciences. That provided good support for entrance into the University of New Mexico as a premed major on scholarship.

But I found the premed required courses incredibly unappealing; I changed to anthropology so I could deal with more interesting questions to me. But that still wasn't what I wanted to do. So I left school, moved to Chicago, and worked in radio for six years. Then I decided I really did want my degree.

This time I went to St. John's, which takes no transfer credits, so I'm a freshman. If I were back at UNM, I'd be a senior. My difficulty with schools like UNM is you get plugged into one track with one major and you are not able to pursue what you are curious about. But that, to me, is the key to education.

High school students should get to try different options. If you aren't sure the college you've chosen is the right one for you, or if you just don't want to be in college, don't panic about the pressure you are going to be under. I can't overemphasize that! Explore all your options; take opportunities; try something out before making a lifelong commitment. Students get told they have to choose right away, but you don't really know what's out there because you haven't been out of school to see. You'll be happiest if you find answers to questions you yourself are interested in.

When I left UNM, I didn't know if I would go back to school. I don't know if a year off would have been long enough. It took me five more years to develop the maturity needed to get the most out of college. Having already started it and knowing what I was getting back into made it not quite so intimidating.

Chris Coucheron-Aamot, St. John's College, Sante Fe, New Mexico

10 Mistakes to Avoid When Choosing a College

1. Your entire group of high school friends is applying to the local college so everyone can still be together.

2. The campus must be near a shopping mall.

3. This is the school your parents attended; they were happy there and are positive you will be too.

4. This college is absolutely the *only* one in the world for you, so you don't bother to investigate others.

5. The school is so close to home that your parents will still do your laundry and feed you a couple times a week.

6. You have almost no firsthand knowledge of or experience with the college, but are betting that the place will be a good match for you.

7. The extracurricular and intramural sports offerings aren't to your liking, but all you intend to do is study for the next four years, so who cares?

8. You'll be the smartest student on campus.

9. It's cheap.

10. Either: You live in a big city; you don't know anything about small towns, so why would you consider a small-town college? Or: You live in a small town; you don't know anything about big cities, so why would you consider a big-city college?

End-of-Chapter Questions

9.1 Why should I consider big schools and small ones at this point? What factors are important to me regarding size?

9.2 How many miles from home is the farthest college that I'm interested in? How many hours to drive? What does an airline ticket cost today?

9.3 What's my experience with being far away from home and family, whether for a short or long time? How many times would I want to come home before the winter holidays?

9.4 How do I function in familiar versus new and different surroundings?

9.5 How many courses specifically in my areas of interest are offered by the different size colleges I have looked at?

9.6 Do I have a major in mind? What draws me to that field? If I don't have a major in mind, am I being pressured to name one? Do I understand why people are pressuring me? Do they understand my point of view?

9.7 Is cost a factor at this point?

9.8 What would be the advantages and disadvantages of considering a faith-based school?

9.9 Have I spoken with anyone who attends a religiously affiliated school?

9.10 What would be the advantages and disadvantages of considering a single gender school? Have I spoken with anyone who attends a single gender school?

9.11 What is the difference between military academies and other colleges? Have I spoken with anyone who went through a military academy?

9.12 How ethnically diverse is the student body and faculty? How important is that to me?

9.13 Are there specific centers or organized groups for the various constituencies on campus—from Democrats and Republicans to gays and lesbians?

9.14 How do I differentiate hearsay from fact when it comes to a school's reputation?

9.15 What kinds of internships do students get in the areas that interest me?

9.16 What is the graduation rate in four years, five years, and six years?

10
SAT, ACT, and Other Tests

Since the United States has no national educational standards, a B in a private, upstate New York school can mean one thing and a B in a rural Mississippi public school can mean another. In fact, a B from Teacher Smith in your high school can mean something entirely different from a B in Teacher Jones's class down the hall. That's why many colleges and universities don't rely solely on GPA and class rank in the admissions process, adding ACT or SAT test scores to the mix. Educators believe these scores reflect not only what you have learned, but also how hard you work and your potential for doing well—or not—in college.

The ACT—or A-C-T—and the new SAT—or S-A-T—are the two national achievement tests colleges uniformly consider in admissions decisions. In fact, most schools don't care which one you take. These tests are aligned with your course work and curriculum, measuring how much you have learned in school. Neither is an aptitude or intelligence test.

The SAT was developed by the Educational Testing Service for the College Board, a nonprofit association of schools, colleges, universities, and educational organizations. The College Board is located in Princeton, New Jersey. Originally, SAT stood for Scholastic Aptitude Test, but now only the letters are officially used. Effective March 2005, the College Board will replace the old SAT I with the new SAT.

The ACT (American College Testing Program) Assessment was developed by the ACT, an independent, not-for-profit organization in Iowa City, Iowa, governed by educators.

About the ACT

- ❏ The ACT has four components: English, reading, mathematics, and science, with 215 multiple-choice questions. A new, optional 30-minute writing test measures the skills taught in high school and expected of students entering first-year college composition courses. Some colleges require the writing test results for admissions and/or course placement purposes, so whether you take the test will be based on the colleges you consider.

- ❏ The ACT takes 2 hours and 55 minutes; add 30 minutes if you're taking the new writing section.

- ❏ Individual scores for each ACT area range from 1 to 36; these scores are averaged into a composite score. If you choose to take the writing test, that score is combined with your English test score. The highest you can score is 36. You'll also receive a writing test subscore and feedback on your essay.

- ❏ ACT scores are mailed within four weeks. Scores are available earlier on the Web for an $8 fee.

- ❏ For more details regarding the ACT Assessment, go to www.act.org.

About the New SAT

- ❏ The SAT has three components: math, critical reading, and writing. An experimental section does not count toward your score. The math section includes Algebra II concepts, as well as functions, more geometry, data analysis, and statistics; quantitative comparisons have been eliminated. The critical reading section focuses on reading comprehension and includes both short and long reading passages; analogies have been eliminated. The writing section includes an essay and multiple-choice grammar questions.

- ❏ The SAT takes 3 hours and 30 minutes.

- ❏ The SAT is scored 200 to 800 writing, 200 to 800 math, and 200 to 800 critical reading. The highest you can score is 2400.

- ❏ SAT scores are mailed within three weeks. You can get your scores earlier on the Web or by phone, although there is an additional $8 fee if you go the phone route.

- ❏ For more details regarding the SAT, go to www.collegeboard.com.

Other Tests

❑ SAT II: Subject Tests measure your knowledge and the ability to apply that knowledge in English, history, math, sciences, and foreign languages. Some colleges, particularly ones that are highly selective, require students to take one or more of these tests, in addition to the SAT, for admission and/or placement in freshman-level courses. You should check with the schools in which you're interested.

❑ The Preliminary SAT/National Merit Scholarship Qualifying Test, or PSAT/NMSQT, gives you an idea of how you might perform on the SAT. The test is required for students wishing to compete for National Merit Scholarships, National Achievement Scholarships for black students, and scholarships from the National Hispanic Scholars Awards Program. Along with other criteria, the PSAT qualifies students who want to be considered for a military academy.

❑ The PLAN is practice for the ACT and, again, will give you an idea of how you might do on the ACT. It also has a substantial career planning component.

❑ AP (Advanced Placement) exams are given after you've completed designated college-level courses in high school. There are 34 courses in 19 subject areas. Depending upon your exam score, many colleges will give you credit for the course. Taking AP courses shows admissions counselors that you're ready for college, willing to push yourself, and committed to academic excellence.

Best Information Sources for Tests

In addition to the SAT and ACT sites, other Web sites include for-profit companies and individuals offering test prep tutorial services. Actually, there's SO MUCH cyberspace information that your guidance counseling office may be the best place to begin the sorting-out process. As you enter the maze of information, it's likely you can get a list of reputable Web sites from your counselor. Also, group meetings, parent nights, and one-on-one conversations should provide you with some direction. Plus, your counseling office may be as good as the public library when it comes to big college guide books and other reference resources.

When to Take the Tests

You can begin taking the tests in junior high, although most students don't start until high school. The later you take a test, the more you will have learned and the higher your score should be.

Generally, the PSAT/NMSQT is taken in sophomore and junior years for SAT practice, and it must be taken in your junior year to be eligible for National Merit Scholarships, other scholarships, and the military academies. The PLAN is also taken sophomore year.

The ACT is given six times a year, in February, April, June, September (but not in all states), October, and December. The SAT is given seven times a year, in January, March or April, May, June, October, November, and December.

Finding Dates and Test Sites

ACT at www.act.org

❑ **Dates:** Click "Next Test Date" to open ACT Assessment Test Dates (within the 50 United States) for the current and next year.

❑ **Sites:** Under Where and When, enter your state and, if you wish, city. You'll find a list of high schools in your city, the Center Code for each school, and the test dates. Notice that testing may not be available at every site on every date.

❑ **Special services:** Click "About the ACT Assessment," then "ACT Registration," and "Special Circumstances" for students with disabilities, non-Saturday testing, state-funded vouchers, fee waivers, homebound or confined students, and for junior high or middle school students.

SAT at www.collegeboard.com

❑ **Dates:** Click "SAT Registration"; click "Calendar & Fees" to view tests given on each date, and the registration deadlines for U.S. Regular, U.S. Late, International Early, and International Regular. Scroll down for test fees; click "More Fees" at page bottom for a complete list of services and fees.

❑ **Sites:** Click "For Students"; "Test Center/Code Search"; "Test Centers." Select a test date, indicate your state and, if you wish, city, and click "Search."

❑ **Special services:** Click "SAT Registration"; click menu items for "Accommodations," "Special Circumstances" for Sunday testing and for those under age 13, or "Students with Disabilities."

There are advantages to testing in your junior year. Test contents are based on your curriculum, so you should have completed the course work corresponding to the test materials by then. Forwarding your results to certain colleges demonstrates your interest in those schools. Their admissions officers can contact you before your senior year and send information about admissions, course placement, scholarships, and special programs. Also, having that information ahead of time can result in more focused campus visits.

You'll also have the results in time to make decisions about senior year courses. If you are weak in science, for example, you may want to take physics or chemistry. And you can retest if you aren't pleased with your scores.

It's best to take an SAT II at the end of the semester in which you studied that particular subject so the information's still fresh. You can only take three a day—and that's plenty. In fact, despite the additional cost, many students choose to take two tests on one day and, if necessary, a third on a separate day so they are rested to do their best.

Register for the Tests

Register via the Internet using the online form, or through regular mail, using a form in the registration packet available free from your counselor. (That registration packet also includes sample tests, by the way.) Online registration files remain active for 72 hours once you've begun. By Internet or paper, it takes between 60 and 90 minutes to complete the registration form and send it with your payment. Either way, the registration deadline will be at least six weeks prior to a test date for the SAT and four weeks prior to a test date for the ACT.

Both organizations may extend their online registration deadlines because of the huge number of people trying to log on. But you risk paying a late fee if they don't extend the deadline. You can even register by phone if you meet the requirements. And, of course, there are lots of exceptions to all of these rules. Best advice? Talk to your counselor or visit the Web sites' FAQ links, which address the most commonly asked questions.

Basic registration fees are $26 ($29 in Florida) for the ACT, with an additional fee for the optional ACT writing test, and $36 to $38 for the SAT. Both registration fees include sending up to four score reports to colleges of your choice. Plus, there are lots of additional options—with fees attached.

Generally, PSAT and PLAN registrations are handled through your counseling office.

How to Register Online

ACT at www.act.org
Click "Register" and then "Online Registration." Read directions on this page and at the bottom click "Online Registration." You will choose your test date and test center, receive immediate registration confirmation, and select a specific number of colleges and universities you'd like your scores forwarded to. If you want scores sent to more schools, there is an additional charge.

SAT at www.collegeboard.com
Click "SAT Registration"; "Register Now." Sign in with your user name and password or sign up as a new member for access to online registration. As with the ACT, above, you will choose your test date and test center, receive immediate registration confirmation, and select colleges and universities you'd like your scores forwarded to. Again, if you want scores sent to more schools, there is an additional charge.

How to Prepare

For starters, memorizing long lists of facts won't do much good because these tests are based on what you've learned—not since the beginning of the semester, but since you started learning. Jeff Rubenstein, vice president at The Princeton Review, says, "A huge issue is with familiarity and comfort. Test day is always going to be a little weird, so the more you can put yourself in a position like test day ahead of time, the more poised you'll be on the actual day. Don't take practice tests in your room. Go to the library, or some other place where you aren't quite comfortable. That will force you to learn how to take the test in an area that isn't quite safe."

What's My Mental Approach to the Tests?

❑ How do I feel about taking tests generally? Am I confident or stressed?

❑ How have I performed on other standardized tests in school?

❑ Can I make a test study-time plan and stick with it?

❑ Do I prefer to study alone or in a group? Should I take a test-prep class?

Sample Questions Online

A Google search for ACT and SAT test prep questions calls up sites that provide sample questions *and* answers, with tips on how to get those answers; sites that offer specific suggestions for how to approach each of the tests' subject areas; and sites that want to sell you their products—ranging from test prep books to test prep online or classroom courses. Many come with a guarantee that your test score will go up, backed by returning your money or a pledge to work with you until your scores improve significantly. Whatever the guarantee, read all the documents or Web pages with the specific rules, and call the company for clarification, in writing, if needed.

How to Prepare Yourself for Test Day

❑ Learn the format and directions ahead of time.

❑ Remember some basic pointers: all questions are worth the same; it doesn't matter how you get the answer but rather that you get it; the right answer to a multiple-choice question is already in front of you.

❑ Take practice tests, including timed practice tests, to give yourself a basic understanding of content, to pinpoint your strengths and weaknesses, and so that you can acquire a sense of the necessary pacing. Plus, you'll see what it feels like to take a really long test.

❑ Get a good night's sleep prior to test day.

❑ That morning, eat a breakfast that will provide enough energy for 3 or 3½ hours of intense concentration.

❑ Dress comfortably and in layers so you'll be okay no matter what the temperature of the testing room.

❑ If you're registered for a national test center, bring your admission ticket.

❑ Bring identification, three sharpened soft-lead No. 2 pencils with good erasers, a wristwatch to pace yourself, and a calculator.

❑ If you aren't familiar with the test center location, leave early. Better yet, take a test run sometime.

There will be distractions, noises you'll have to ignore. That kind of preparation will help you be calmer on test day."

Rubenstein adds that one wrong answer won't make or break the test. "It's very easy to obsess over a question you had two hours earlier," he says. "Let it go." And he agrees that the more you know about the test process ahead of time, the better. That, in fact, is the best preparation.

So practice, practice, practice. Students in the school orchestra practice for the public performance. Basketball players practice before the season-opening game. Test takers should practice before showing up with their No. 2 pencils on test day.

Test Preparation Classes

The two big test creators—the ACT and the College Board for its SAT—offer test preparation materials online, in books, and through the counseling office. The two big test prep companies, however, are Kaplan, Inc., and Princeton Review. They offer online and on-site test prep classes as well as private tutoring, books, and software for the ACT, PSAT, the SAT, and SAT II: Subject Tests.

Test prep companies offer lessons on test-taking skills, drills, practice tests, timed tests, and detailed score reports that indicate your areas of weakness. You can focus on the test in general or—for the PSAT, ACT, and SAT—concentrate on a particular subject. Your test preparation can

Pro versus Con for Test Prep Classes

Pro: Your score likely will go up, depending on the quality of the prep classes. You'll understand the kinds of questions on the test, develop a strategy for answering questions, save time reading directions, and feel more comfortable having practiced. If you are competing for admission against students who take a prep course, you may be at a disadvantage by passing on the option.

Con: Because the tests measure what you have learned in school, commercial test preparation classes aren't necessary if you've been taking the right courses, work hard, and do well academically. Information about content, format, sample questions, and tests as well as what to expect on test day is often available online for free or through your counseling office.

How Good Test Preparation Paid Off

Spence is a college preparatory school. Teak [a fellowship program that helps economically disadvantaged but intellectually gifted students] introduced me to private schools. I didn't know they existed before.

I took the PSAT in the fall of my junior year but I didn't prepare, just took it. I did okay. Then I took practice SATs at home from books and timed myself. I got bad scores and didn't understand why. I had problems with the math especially. I was doing trig and was so removed from ninth grade math that I couldn't remember anything. Most definitely, I thought I needed help.

Teak had weekly prep classes. We'd go over math, basic algebra, and geometry. Also, we were assigned 20 words a week to memorize for the vocabulary section. And we learned about SAT tricks, like instead of just gridding in your answers, write them down for a whole page, then grid them all at once. It saves time. They also taught us how to answer questions by a process of elimination.

I took the SAT in March of my junior year and got 700 on the verbal and 670 on the math. I thought I could do better, so I took it again in November and got 710 on the verbal and 720 on the math.

The test isn't as hard as people think. What gets people in trouble is they wait until the last minute to prepare. They take the practice test the week before. You should start three months before. The more practice tests you do, the better you get. Train yourself to think the way people who made the SAT think. Pace yourself. Get to know your weaknesses and work on them.

It's good to have a tutor because you have someone to guide you, but you don't have to have one. My brother took the SAT and used the test prep books and did better than I did.

Dyese Taylor, Spence Girls School, Manhattan, New York

be adjusted, depending on how much time remains before the real test day. Each test prep company approaches test prep with a little variation. For instance, Peterson's combines skill-building techniques with a personalized curriculum for each student. A student takes a diagnostic test to see how he or she performs on every question and skill tested. Then, an individual instruction program is created, geared to that student's strengths, weaknesses, learning style, and score goals. The end result for any test prep company, individual, or after-school class is not to make you significantly smarter, but to make you a better test taker.

Who takes test prep classes? Students aiming for highly selective colleges and with family incomes sufficient to cover course costs are more likely to take them. Students from disadvantaged schools, areas of the country where most students aim for state or not highly selective colleges, or whose families do not have the ability to pay the big bucks for prep courses do not take them.

Five Key Mistakes to Avoid

1. Spending too much time on a difficult question. Each question is worth the same number of points, so answer all the easy questions first, then come back to the harder questions.

2. Not guessing. You do not get penalized for wrong answers. If you don't know an answer, guess *intelligently*. Leaving a question blank costs as many points as guessing incorrectly.

3. Trying to identify the right answer first. The test is multiple-choice. You can logically eliminate incorrect answers, then make an educated best guess about the remaining options.

4. Making careless mistakes. True, this is a timed test, but you still need to read thoroughly and carefully. And if you must erase, erase thoroughly.

5. Spending too much time on a few problems. Pace yourself, using the watch you have on. You'll also be told when there are five minutes remaining.

Test Scores and Selectivity

Although colleges list the median/range of test scores for their students, many schools say those scores are not the most important factor in an application file. Rather, it's your high school record. Smaller institutions place more importance on GPA, looking at curriculum difficulty, quality of high school, and recommendations.

Then there are the highly selective schools. Yale University in New Haven, Connecticut, receives about 15,000 applicants and admits about 13 percent, which is around 2,000 students. Such schools look at your

Questions to Ask My Counselor

❑ When is the PSAT/NMSQT going to be given here?

❑ Should I take it my sophomore year as practice for when the score really counts in junior year?

❑ Is this school a testing center for the SAT or ACT or will I need to go somewhere nearby?

❑ Do you have any after-school or evening test prep sessions planned?

❑ Where do my scores fit regarding state, private, and highly selective colleges?

❑ Can you steer me toward schools where I will find appropriate academic challenges?

❑ If I have problems while taking the ACT or SAT—I didn't understand directions, perhaps, or I didn't feel well—or if I'm not satisfied with my scores, should I consider retesting?

success in and out of the classroom—grades, school and community activities, special talents, and employment history. But because students applying to selective schools almost always bring good school records with them, the test scores can help shape a decision about whether to admit.

The larger the college, the more important the test scores usually are. That's because their application pool is so big that admissions counselors couldn't possibly begin choosing next year's class by considering everything in each applicant's folder. Nevertheless, the University of California, with branches throughout the state and well over 100,000 students collectively, has adopted a comprehensive or holistic review to assess students on more than objective numbers.

Test scores are also used to award scholarships—including the National Merit Scholarship—as well as to determine merit aid, college class placement, NCAA athletic eligibility, and admittance to a military academy.

How to Rate My SAT/ACT Scores

❑ In those big guidebooks, look at colleges' academic competitiveness, which can range from "admits under 50 percent of applicants" to "open admission." Compare your grades, class rank, and standardized test scores with schools in which you're interested.

❑ Check individual college Web sites for score ranges for the incoming freshman class. That will give you a sense of what schools you should consider.

❑ Ask your counselor where your test scores fall in terms of colleges you are interested in. Are you high, low, or in the middle?

Colleges That Don't Require SAT/ACT

Some colleges and universities make admissions decisions about some applicants without using the SAT or ACT. Practice varies from not requiring any applicants to submit test scores to exempting students who meet grade point average or class rank criteria. Other schools require SAT or ACT scores but use them only for class placement purposes or to conduct research studies.

Such schools often voice concerns that reliance on standardized test scores may negatively impact race and gender equity. Another concern is that test-coaching programs may artificially boost the scores of students who can afford them.

End-of-Chapter Questions

10.1 What is the difference between the new SAT and the ACT?

10.2 What is the SAT II? Do I take the SAT II the same day as the new SAT?

10.3 How do I know which tests are required by colleges in which I am interested?

10.4 When should I take the tests? Can I retake the tests if I don't score well?

10.5 How should I prepare to take the tests? Are test prep classes recommended by my counselor?

10.6 Are test prep classes just for those aiming for highly selective colleges? If I'm not going to a highly selective school, how can a test prep class benefit me?

10.7 Where can I find online information about the ACT and SAT? The PSAT/NMSQT and PLAN tests?

10.8 When should I take the PSAT and/or PLAN tests? Will my counselor automatically tell me or should I ask?

10.9 Have I talked to my counselor about any of these standardized tests?

10.10 How do I register for the SAT and ACT?

10.11 How long do I have to wait before I can get my score? Can I get it online or only by mail?

Part **3**
Making the Big Decision

11

Campus Tours Make a Difference

You'll accumulate plenty of information about colleges via Web surfing. But to get a real feel for a school, nothing comes close to actually walking the campus and talking to people you meet.

If the schools you're thinking about are far from home, ask your parents to consider making the campus visit part of a road trip. Driving from home to campus provides a sense of distance you can't get by flying. And for college freshmen, distance from home can be a very big deal.

Life's different in different parts of the country. Customs, weather, pace, and even people's speech and demeanor vary from region to region. Spending time on a faraway campus gives you a valuable sneak preview.

If the schools you're considering are so close to home that you've been on campus before, take the group tour anyway. You'll learn different things about the school than when you went to a basketball game, enrolled in a summer class, or attended a rock concert on campus. With the tour and your informal experiences, you'll have a better picture of whether this is the place you want to live and learn for the next four years.

If your trips coincide with high school holidays—perhaps fall or spring break—you won't miss your classes. But if you visit the campuses when their classes are in session, you can see what really goes on. The atmosphere is different on weekends, during summer school, or spring break, when most students are gone. A good visit without staying overnight in a dormitory takes three-plus hours. Two campuses a day are plenty.

Who, if anyone, should accompany you? Should you tour with your family? With a friend? Counselors and admissions officers realize most high school students would prefer to tour campus with friends rather than family. That said, they strongly suggest you do the touring with family because you want to select the college that fits *you* best. That means your visit should be free of the distracting influence of friends. In the end, if a friend has the same match as you, so be it.

How to Plan Your Tour

Campus tours are not conducted all day, every day, so figure out your time frame for visits and sign up. (You can always cancel and try to reschedule if your plans change.)

You can also call the admissions office to sign up for a visit. For anything beyond the generic group tour, call several months ahead. Ask what the tour includes. If something important to you is not included in the tour—seeing the wellness facility, checking out handicap accessibility, or talking with the soccer coach, for example—ask if that can be arranged. Also, give serious consideration to:

❏ Sitting in on a class in your area of interest. You can observe whether the professor lectures or leads a discussion and if students appear bored or involved. You can visit with a couple of students to find out what they think of the department and professors.

❏ Meeting a professor in your area of interest. If you get this opportunity, have some questions ready because discussion time may be limited.

❏ Staying overnight in the dorm. This should yield the real scoop on what students think about parties, classes, professors, administration, activities, food—everything. That's what happens when you have a good host who is candid, introduces you to other students, and makes sure your stay is pleasant. If you get a poor host (it happens), you'll probably go home and cross that college off your list.

Some colleges offer a day of in-depth activities for your visit—for a fee. Among the activities in the University of Arizona's UA101 ($15 fee), you'll meet students and faculty, learn about housing options, freshman programs, tour the campus, and have lunch. The university also offers a less

---

 Scheduling Tours

Many college sites offer fast, easy scheduling for visits. Some sites list Campus Visits on the front page; others tuck Campus Visits within categories such as Admissions, Undergraduate Admissions, Prospective Students, or Future Students. The model path: www.abracadabrau.edu/Prospective Students/Visit/Schedule a Visit.

What to Look For on My Tour

- ❏ The size of the dorm rooms
- ❏ Location of the laundry, kitchen, dining, and workout facilities
- ❏ Distance from the dorm to classrooms and labs (How do you feel about a 15-minute jaunt in a 15-degree wind chill or 110-degree heat?)
- ❏ Library hours, noise, seating, and access to materials
- ❏ Campus security measures such as good lighting, a process for allowing strangers into a dorm, and a visible security force
- ❏ People smiling and interacting or absorbed and in a hurry
- ❏ Information posted on bulletin boards, posters and fliers—all excellent indicators of what interests students
- ❏ The makes of cars parked on campus (Are there more Fords or Ferraris?)

extensive free tour that includes major buildings, a residence hall, and the campus lore.

Freshman Living Arrangements

An important aspect of the tour is a walk through the dorms. Because many colleges require out-of-town students to live in assigned housing as freshmen, a (probably quite small) room or suite will become your home away from home. It's important to feel comfortable in the surroundings.

What should you look for when it comes to campus housing, and what kinds of questions should you ask? Here are a few things to consider:

- ❏ How are freshmen assigned to dorms?
- ❏ Can I choose my roommate or are roommates assigned?
- ❏ Are special-interest floors, wings, or houses available to freshmen?
- ❏ What about study hours? Smoking? Overnight guests?
- ❏ Is housing provided—or even required—beyond freshman year?
- ❏ What happens if there are more freshmen enrolled than dorm space available?

What to Ask about Computers

- ❏ Are there publicly accessible kiosks for checking your e-mail, CNN, and other sites? Is there a fee?
- ❏ Is there Web access to e-mail (such as Hotmail, AOL, or the school's site)?
- ❏ What services does the library subscribe to that you can use without a fee from your residence room?
- ❏ Is the speed of the network adequate so you do not have long waits for online searches?
- ❏ Is wireless an option on campus? If so, where exactly?
- ❏ Is there a specifically required computer and software for the engineering or other schools?
- ❏ How do professors use online resources for classes? Do professors have syllabi, notes, PowerPoints, assignments, or interactive discussions available online?
- ❏ What is the policy regarding computer use for nonacademic interests?

Computers

No surprise here: Technology will play a vital role in your college education, no matter what your major. So a school's computer facilities, including Internet access, are very important. Some campuses have a wireless network so that with installation of the appropriate wireless card and software, you can use your laptop to access e-mail and the Internet from various places such as a library study table, dining hall, or classroom. Make sure the school can meet your specific computing needs whether you are aiming for graphic design, political science, or physics.

Be aware too that the college is not like home, where you might download basically at will. Colleges have policies delineating appropriate use, and they often limit how much you can download.

Why Your Tour Guide May Affect Your Decision

Guides or "ambassadors" are students who were at one time prospective students like you. They can tell you about their experiences with environment and classes. Ask the guide questions—and remember, there is no stupid question, and the guide does not evaluate you for admission.

Two good questions: What surprised you most when you arrived as a freshman? What do you wish you'd found out about the school when you were a prospective student here? You may also have specific issues you'd like addressed: the prevalence of drugs and alcohol, the library's adequacy, how strictly campus rules are enforced, the balance between academics and a social life. Expect honest answers, but realize that the guide is probably getting paid to conduct the tour. So asking the same questions of students you meet randomly is a good idea.

Choosing a College Based on a Major Professor

When I first started looking at colleges, I had no idea what Oberlin even was. I was looking at several, including Northwestern. The viola professor, Peter Slowik, was there, and I was interested in him because my brother Adam was studying with him.

During my freshman year in high school I had auditioned and gotten accepted to a music festival at Northwestern. While there, I saw how Professor Slowik taught and was able to have a lesson with him. I knew then that I really wanted to study with him, but didn't think I could get into Northwestern because my ACT scores weren't high enough. But my junior year in high school, Professor Slowik and my brother both transferred to Oberlin, so I put it on my list. When I went there to visit, I got a lesson with Professor Slowik, and that helped when audition time came, because he could see progress.

I trusted my brother's judgment that Oberlin would be good for me. He said it would be competitive. You always have to put yourself out there; the more competition, the more you learn.

Besides the normal application process, I had to go back to Oberlin the fall of my senior year to audition. Professor Slowik already knew me, and I was already comfortable playing in front of him.

If you feel comfortable with a professor, feel like you're going to learn, you know you're choosing the right school. If you have been playing for a while, then you know who will be good for you and not good for you.

Abby Meyer, Oberlin (Ohio) College, Conservatory of Music

What Did I Learn on My Campus Visit . . .

from the Admissions Officer?
❑ Did the admissions officer answer all my questions?
❑ If not, will that person help me find answers once I'm home again?
❑ Do the take-home materials seem helpful?
❑ Were the other employees in the admissions office student-friendly?

from the Tour Guide?
❑ Did he or she answer all my questions?
❑ Did the guide seem spontaneous and enthusiastic or did the presentation sound scripted?
❑ Did the guide provide a sense of what life is like on campus?
❑ Did the guide include all—or almost all—major points of interest in the tour?

from Visiting a Class?
❑ Was the professor respectful of students?
❑ Did the students pay attention in class?
❑ Did they use laptops?
❑ If a lab was included, was the equipment up-do-date?

from Spending the Night in a Dorm?
❑ Was the host enthusiastic and pleased to be at the school?
❑ Did the host introduce me to other students and provide time for me to talk?
❑ Was the experience worth my time?

The guide (or admissions office where you meet the guide) will probably have a folder of materials for you to take home. If a campus newspaper isn't included, ask for one so you can see what's going on. Newspaper quality varies widely from campus to campus and is only a snapshot of one day or week on campus. Still, it may give you another indication of student and administration attitudes.

Jot down your thoughts about the school as soon as possible after each campus tour. Visiting several campuses before actually listing the pluses and minuses of each school can make for muddled evaluations.

My Scorecard after the Campus Tour

On a scale of A (Definitely yes), B (Could be happy here), C (Don't know), D (Not so good), and F (Definitely no):

The distance from home to school: _____

The "feel" of the campus: _____

The dorm and other campus buildings: _____

The people with whom I talked: _____

The school overall: _____

Choosing a College Based on a Campus Visit

When I began thinking about going off to college, I wanted to stay close to home. My family is very close-knit and I was offered large scholarships to go to state schools in Iowa. The summer before my senior year, my family took a road trip to New England to visit some of my mother's relatives. On our way home, we stopped at Cornell University in New York because my mother had earned her master's degree there. Upon arrival, I realized that this university was unlike any school I had seen close to home. Not only did it have stellar academics, but also breathtaking scenery, a world-renowned faculty, and a great scholastic atmosphere.

In mid-October of my senior year, coincidentally, my father had a meeting in Syracuse, only about an hour's drive from Cornell. I ended up visiting Cornell for three days, staying overnight at one of the dorms with a great host. I was able to attend some classes, take tours of the campus, and talk with students about what Cornell was really like. After my trip, I knew that I wanted to attend Cornell.

I ended up applying Early Decision to Cornell, and when I was accepted into the biological and environmental engineering program, I felt extremely lucky that I had visited the campus and I knew I'd made the right decision.

Gwen Owens, Cornell University, Ithaca, New York

End-of-Chapter Questions

11.1 Do I have access to college tour trips sponsored by businesses, my high school, or particular colleges?

11.2 What's my high school's policy on being absent to visit colleges? During my campus tour trips, how will I keep up with my homework?

11.3 Since our first contact, has the college admissions office consistently been helpful in planning my visit?

11.4 If I'm an athlete, have I arranged to meet with the appropriate coach? If I'm in an extracurricular activity (debate or drama, for example), do arrangements include the opportunity to meet with the appropriate faculty person?

11.5 If I have a particular interest (leadership opportunities or playing bassoon in the band, for example), do arrangements include the opportunity to meet with a student who is pursuing that interest on campus?

11.6 If I require special services (hearing or visually impaired, handicap accessibility, learning disabilities), do arrangements include the opportunity to inquire about these accommodations?

11.7 During the tour, did students, staff, and professors seem friendly, reserved, or not interested in each other?

11.8 What do the buildings look like—inside and out? Are freshmen guaranteed dorm space?

11.9 What about health center staffing, hours, services? Are visits covered by insurance?

11.10 Does the Greek system dominate the campus, share space with Independents, or is it even visible?

11.11 How's the dining hall food? Are there options for various dietary needs and preferences?

11.12 If my heart's set on a profession that requires a graduate degree (doctor, lawyer, research biologist, for example), how many of the college's students get into graduate programs, and where? (No, it's not too early to consider those scenarios!)

11.13 Is the community surrounding the campus appealing?

11.14 Whatever the campus atmosphere—liberal, conservative, serious, laid-back, straight, funky—did I feel comfortable?

11.15 Did it seem to be a party school? Are there Friday and/or Saturday classes?

11.16 Are the school and I a good match academically, so I'm neither bored nor chained to the library 24 hours a day?

11.17 Is it appropriate for me to call or e-mail the college admissions officer with any additional questions?

11.18 Can I discern important differences among the colleges I visited?

11.19 What three things do I like best about each school? Give an example for each.

11.20 What three things do I like least about each school? Give an example for each.

12
The Campus Interview

The one-on-one interview is almost like an endangered species—rare and vulnerable to extinction. Because of the large volume of applications and/or admission being based strictly on numbers (standardized test scores, GPA, and/or class rank), one-on-one interviews may not be required and, in truth, may even be discouraged.

It's easy to see why: if a school receives 10,000 applications and an interview takes 30 minutes, that's 5,000 hours spent just during interviews—more than two years of 40-hour workweeks!

Group Interviews

Instead of one-on-one interviews, many colleges offer group information sessions that often include a question-and-answer time. The admissions representative will answer general questions (from parents as well as students) about financial aid, scholarships, environment, number of students in freshman English sections, special services, intramurals—anything to do with the college experience. The representative will not, however, be able to address personal situations. For example, if your parents earn $100,000 a year, should your family apply for financial aid? You'll have to make an appointment with the financial aid office for such a specific query.

Depending upon the size of your group, you may have an opportunity to leave a good impression with the admissions representative based on your questions or comments. These group sessions, though, are not related to the personal interview and don't impact individual evaluations. In fact, the representative usually does not ask your name.

When you're making arrangements for the campus tour, ask about attending a group interview during the same visit.

How Can a One-on-One Help Me?

Many highly selective schools and small, private colleges still conduct personal interviews. They usually last from 30 to 60 minutes. If a college you're interested in either recommends or calls an interview "optional," do the interview. Your effort indicates strong interest to the college, which is a plus for admission.

Whether you consider a college as a "safety" (admission is almost always automatic), "maybe" (not a sure thing but your numbers match the college's profile), or a "reach" (even though qualified, you cannot count on getting in), the interview is the best opportunity for the real *live* you to make a positive impression on the admissions officer. Until you've been offered admission to a particular school and accepted the offer, each school is important.

How Does the Interview Work?

You'll find the interview to be a two-way street: The school wants to know more about you, but the school also wants you to know more about it. Because every school wants the best students, the person interviewing you will try to impress you with the school's virtues. That can be a real confidence booster.

Although it's not meant to be, this one-on-one interview—just you and the admissions representative—may sound a bit threatening. So think of it more in terms of an exchange of information: First, the admissions officer will ask you questions. During the interview, you should have an opportunity to ask questions too. But don't ask ones to which you should already know the answer, such as, "Do you have a Spanish language major?" or "What are your graduate schools?"

The interview is also an opportunity to give the admissions representative personal information regarding your record and abilities that would otherwise be unavailable or difficult to understand. You might want to explain that poor grades during a particular semester were due to an illness or death in the family, for example, or that you dropped out of the basketball program because you wanted to devote as much time as possible to drama. Naturally, whatever you say should be accurate.

How the admissions officer's evaluation is used differs from one campus to another. The evaluation may encourage the admissions officer to advocate for you during meetings to discuss applicants. In some cases, the interview may be considered as the school looks at merit-based grant and scholarship opportunities.

How Can I Prepare for the Interview?

What do I want the college rep to remember about me?

Limit yourself to three points, then build your responses—as well as your own questions—around that vision.

What should I do if I don't understand what the interviewer means by a particular question?

Simply request that the person repeat the question, and acknowledge that you don't understand what he or she is asking for. Interviewers are more impressed when you admit to not understanding something than when you try to bluff.

Are rapid-fire responses always best?

Not necessarily. If a response isn't on the tip of your tongue, take time to think about your answer. A bit of thoughtful silence is okay.

Are simple "Yes" or "No" responses to an interviewer's questions okay?

Rarely. The more the interviewer knows about you, the better. Think about examples or anecdotes to include in your answers: things you've accomplished, a favorite teacher, class, activity, book, or movie. If a "Yes" or "No" response fits the question, tell the interviewer why you chose that response.

Should I memorize my responses?

No. Think about your possible responses but memorizing will make your answers sound scripted rather than spontaneous.

What should I wear to the interview?

That depends on your style and the type of school. You'd probably dress differently for an interview at an Ivy League school than you would for an interview at the Kansas City Art Institute. It's important you feel comfortable, but think about it: Clothes make the first impression, which is partly why you are doing this interview to begin with.

Some schools don't include any evaluation of the interview within the admissions discussions. Rather, they see the interview as an opportunity for you to become familiar with the college and have your questions answered. A good interview, however, can never hurt you.

Sample Responses to Questions You May Be Asked

Tell me about your family.

Poor Answer: *There's not much to tell. There's my parents and little brother.*

Impressive Answer (because it's truthful and kind with a specific example): *I have my parents and just one little brother. Sometimes he's kind of a pest because he wants to hang out with me when my friends come over. But he's really funny too. He can imitate cartoon characters perfectly. Maybe he'll be a stand-up comic one day.*

Tell me about your high school.

This doesn't mean everything about the school, but where do you start? Begin with the part of school that pertains to one of those three main points you want the interviewer to remember about you. If your strength is leadership, talk about the many opportunities not only academically but also in extracurricular activities to develop leadership skills, learn to work with a group, and make a difference. Then tell about the food drive where your group collected a significant amount of items.

What is one of your favorite things to do?

Poor Answer: *I like to watch TV or rent DVDs.*

Impressive Answer (short, the activity is challenging and you tell what you learned): *I really liked the triathlon I did for the first time last spring. I was scared I wouldn't finish because I'm not much of a runner, but I like to swim and bike. I practiced and did okay. It helped me know I can do new things at college.* If you really do like TV and DVDs, tell what you get out of a particular program that helps you in school, in dealing with other people or deciding what you want to do with your life.

Who is your hero?

Pick someone dead or alive, famous or obscure, rich or not so rich, male or female. Describe some action that the person has done or accomplished. Then tell why that action is important to you or others and what you might do as a result of the action.

Why did you choose to visit our college?

Poor Answer: *Well, it's close to home and my folks don't want me to go too far away.*

Impressive Answer (aligns with one of the school's strengths and piggybacks a question for you to get information): *I'm interested in journalism and your Web site indicated you have a new communications center with state-of-the-art equipment. Do you expect an increase in the number of journalism majors because of the new facility? How do you think the new building will affect students?*

What other schools are on your list?

Interviewers expect you to comparison shop. But there is little to be gained by sharing your list. Finesse the question with truthful answers such as you have similar colleges on the list, you are undecided, or you do not feel comfortable answering that question.

What are your biggest accomplishments? Your strengths? Weaknesses? Are you creative? A leader? Organized? Intellectually curious?

Poor Answer: *Some people say I'm disorganized and I guess I do put things off a lot.*

Impressive Answer (deals positively with a trait that could have negative results): *Some people think I'm disorganized. I'm pretty random, but that approach works for me. I meet assignment deadlines and my grades are good.*

What have been some of your goals? Have you reached them? What are your goals now?

Poor Answer: *I want to go to college.*

Impressive Answer (shows thought and asks a question to keep the conversation going): *In high school it's been more like get the research paper done, then do the chemistry project, then something else. Now I'm thinking I'd like to own my own business one day. I like math and figuring out how to do things. I'd like to work for someone else first to get experience. Are there part-time jobs like that on campus?*

If you are admitted here, what can you contribute to this college?

You probably think in terms of what the college will do for you. But interviewers are looking for students who will make the college better because of their presence.

Impressive Answer: *Our family has been involved in volunteer work with the homeless since I was little, and this past summer I babysat in a women's shelter. I want to continue that kind of work while in college, and your school has a reputation for community outreach opportunities that appeal to me.*

Sample Questions for the Admissions Officer

1. I'm interested in environmental studies. What makes your program stronger than those at other schools?

2. How many times can I change my major and still graduate in four years? Or five years?

3. Am I likely to graduate in four years if I don't change my major? What is the average number of years to graduate? (FYI, some students take six years without changing their major.)

4. Are there really 275 students in a freshman English class? (Often, yes. Sometimes there are more.) Are there enough sections for all who want the class that semester?

5. Follow-up question: Is that basic class required for all students or will my good grades in English let me take a different English class?

6. Do graduate students or professors teach freshman classes? (It's not unusual for graduate students to teach freshmen. That gives grad students classroom experience, plus they cost less than professors. Still, they have neither the experience nor the knowledge of a full professor.)

7. What percentage of students participates in extracurricular activities? Social events? Intramurals? Internship opportunities?

8. What do students do on weekends? (At some schools many students leave en masse every weekend. You'll probably spend most weekends on campus, though, and you don't want to study *all* the time, do you?)

9. How are roommates assigned? What if the pairing doesn't work out?

If giving you a chance to ask questions doesn't seem to be part of the admissions officer's routine, you can easily create the opportunity. When there's a break in the conversation, simply say, "May I ask you a couple of questions?"

Auditions and Portfolios

If you're applying to a performance-based conservatory, it would not be unusual to be required to audition in addition to an interview. Students studying music may be asked to play a major work and scales. Drama students may perform and, possibly, handle a cold reading.

Visual arts and film students may be asked to present a portfolio in person or send it to the school for evaluation. If no request is made, you may include a small portfolio with your application and ask that the admissions office forward it to the head of the relevant department. In any case, send copies rather than original materials. Requirements, which differ

What the Interview Was Really Like

The interview is a great chance for people to figure out who you really are and not just what's on paper. I could bring up things important to me but not highlighted in my application. Plus it was a good opportunity to talk to someone about the school.

Interviewers often ask questions about your high school experience. It's a good idea to think about what you liked and didn't like or what was hard and easy about high school. They don't ask complicated questions about your political issues or anything like that, but often they'll ask questions that help them understand your ideas and values. I had one interviewer ask who was a role model in my life. Everyone asked what I did in the summer because it shows what you do with your free time. I did programs in marine biology and oceanography. I also talked about singing, which is not an academic interest and therefore not highlighted in my application. But I sang in my church and high school and organized groups that sang in nursing homes, so it was important to me.

Every interviewer will ask if you have questions about the school, so have them ready. That shows you have serious interest. I asked about the choral program, science offerings, or even about social life. It's a great time to have a one-on-one conversation about the school.

My Bates interviewer was a senior who'd trained with admissions. I was interviewed by senior admissions fellows at several interviews. It was nice to talk to a current student; I felt like I could ask about all aspects of the school and get real answers.

Most of the time, you and the interviewer are in chairs or on a couch in a conversation setting. They lasted 30 to 45 minutes. I wore nice, casual clothes. It's an informal thing, but you don't want to show up in jeans and a T-shirt. Most girls wore nice pants or a skirt and sweater, and guys wore khaki pants and a button-down shirt.

Christine Fletcher, Bates College, Lewiston, Maine

from one institution to another, should be included with the school's recruitment information.

Do Parents Go to the Interview Too?

Parents going into the interview with you is like having them tag along on your prom date. Parents can wait in the reception area. When the interview is over, the interviewer may return with you to the reception area and meet your parents.

They may have questions for the admissions staff about certain school policies—perhaps the procedure for grade notification, availability of service learning opportunities, or health care—questions you may not have considered yet. Check with the admissions office when setting up your interview to find out when parents may ask such questions. Other appointments to coordinate are with financial aid and, if applicable, services for special needs students.

Evaluate Your Performance

After each one-on-one meeting, think about what you did well and what you can change for future interviews. Were you caught off guard by any questions? As with your campus tour, jot down notes before you go home. When you get back home, you may come up with questions you wish you had asked. In that case, contact the admissions officer again.

Finally, once you have pulled together all the information from your interviews and campus tours, you should have a sense about where each school now fits on your list of possibilities.

Other Interview Options

If you can't interview on campus, you have two options: attend the college information meeting at your high school and speak informally with the admissions representative or request an interview with one of the alumni (graduates of the college) in your hometown. The graduate will contact you to set up a meeting in a public place such as the person's office or a coffee shop. The interview will be similar to an on-campus interview with conversational questions and answers. A prompt thank-you note is definitely appropriate. Although hometown interviews usually are not billed as evaluations, you can leave a strong impression so the interviewer may advocate admission.

Just like the on-campus interview, parents should not be part of any meeting with hometown alumni. Additionally, be sure to follow the same evaluation procedure afterward that you would use for an on-campus interview.

How I Interviewed Off Campus with Alumnae

I did alumnae interviews for Duke and Georgetown [University] applications. They were informative and fun to do.

During information sessions, Duke suggested doing alumni interviews. They said if you do really well, it can help you, but if the interview doesn't confirm what your application says, they'll take your application over one person's opinion in an interview. So something totally out of character won't destroy your chances of admission. It's voluntary, so the application is much more important.

The interviews took about 30 minutes. For the Georgetown one, I went to a lady's house. Typically, interviews are not at a person's house but she had just had a baby. She asked multiple times if I was okay with that. For the Duke interview, we met at a Starbucks. I wore slacks and a collared shirt—not fancy, but I didn't wear jeans. She also dressed casually on the same level, respectful but not dressy.

It wasn't intimidating at all. It was more a conversation about preparation for school, what I did in high school, what I was interested in, what I wanted to do for college. Basically, I said I was going to figure it out here [at Duke]. It was an honest answer. The most fun question was about books. I really like to read so it was interesting to hear her favorites in high school and then mine. She had read all the Harry Potter books and so had I. We talked about the Harry Potter phenomenon and why we thought that had caught on.

I wanted to go to Duke, and the interview made me think more highly of the school. The interview relieved my concerns about Duke's possible homogeneity. My interviewer had very different interests from mine and it was great to see the broad spectrum of students Duke attracts.

Julia Lacy, Duke University, Durham, North Carolina

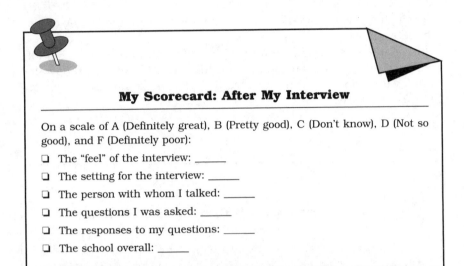

My Scorecard: After My Interview

On a scale of A (Definitely great), B (Pretty good), C (Don't know), D (Not so good), and F (Definitely poor):

❏ The "feel" of the interview: _____
❏ The setting for the interview: _____
❏ The person with whom I talked: _____
❏ The questions I was asked: _____
❏ The responses to my questions: _____
❏ The school overall: _____

End-of-Chapter Questions

12.1 How do I find out whether a school offers one-on-one interviews?

12.2 How far ahead do I need to make an appointment for the interview?

12.3 Do I know the date and time of my interview? Do I know how to get to the interview, including where to park? Where will my parents be during the interview?

12.4 Have I developed a vision of myself that I want to leave with the admissions officer? Do most of the points I want to make tie in with that vision?

12.5 Am I prepared to talk about what I've gained from my involvement in extracurricular activities or athletics? How can I put my best self forward without sounding cocky or like a braggart?

12.6 If I have experienced a particularly traumatic event, is there a counselor, teacher, parent, or other adult in my life who can help me decide whether or how to incorporate that into the interview?

12.7 How do I respond to open-ended or ambiguous questions such as, "What would you most like to accomplish?" and "What do you hope you're doing five years from now?"

12.8 Can I articulate why this particular school is of interest to me?

12.9 Should I practice interviewing ahead of time? Should I memorize answers?

12.10 If the admissions officer doesn't offer me a chance to ask questions, what should I do?

12.11 If there is information I've promised to send to the school after I get back home, do I have a mailing address and correct spelling of the recipient's name and title?

12.12 If I can't get a one-on-one interview, will a group interview be worth my time?

12.13 Have I sent a thank you note to the representative within a week of my visit or interview?

13
Applications:
So Much to Do!

Okay, it's crunch time—either you fill out college applications now or, as one parent told her procrastinating son, "There's always the Army, Navy, and Marines calling."

Fortunately, the list of colleges to which you apply should be shorter than the list of colleges you've been considering. That's because you've visited Web sites, toured campuses, and talked to friends in college and high school as you tried to match your needs and wants with what each college offers. Now you can narrow the application list to a manageable size.

What's a manageable size? Fifteen colleges? Eight? Six? Two? The answer depends on you. Are you fairly confident of getting into your hands-down favorite college? Or is your goal to get into *any* college? There is a big difference! One guideline is the so-called Rule of Twos: apply to two "safe" schools where admission is almost automatic; two "maybe" schools where admission isn't a sure thing but the student-school match looks good; and two "reach" schools, such as highly competitive schools.

For those highly competitive schools, admission decisions may seem based on a roll of the dice. For instance, one student with a 4.5 weighted GPA, perfect ACT score and activities was not admitted to Harvard, but his brother with lesser credentials had been admitted the previous year. The message clearly is to apply to those elite schools if your grades and scores indicate you fall within their parameters. But also apply to less competitive schools, as well as one of your state colleges that does not require an essay or recommendations.

Making Sure I'm Accepted Somewhere

I applied to Vassar because my mom and aunt went here. Mom thought I should at least look at the school, and my aunt has been trying to get me to go here since I was born. I also knew Vassar was a very good school.

I refused to apply to any school that didn't have a Japanese program. I wanted to double major in English and Japanese, and I wanted to go to a small liberal arts school because I'd get lost in a big school. I'm not the kind of person who enjoys anonymity, and I don't want to be just another number.

I also applied to Smith, Grinnell, Macalester, Drake University, and the University of Iowa. The Iowa application was one page that Iowa had already filled out because I'd sent my SAT scores there. I knew I'd be accepted at Iowa, so I'd be going to college even if I didn't get into the schools I wanted.

I like the diversity and the atmosphere of the campus—Vassar was the most ethnically diverse college I applied to. It's a really tightly knit school. It has a sense of community and camaraderie that most schools don't have.

Rachel Lenz of Vassar College, Poughkeepsie, New York

The Common Application

The Web site www.commonapp.org will tell you which colleges require the Common Application exclusively (e.g., Amherst College and Denison University) and those for which it is optional but accepted (e.g., University of Tulsa and Spelman College). You'll be able to complete and e-mail the application or print the form and fill it out by hand to send by regular mail. The FAQ answers questions ranging from cost to how to include your résumé.

Many students apply to 10 or more schools. Why? More students may be applying to schools ranked highly in the annual *U.S. News* ranking of best colleges. Also, multiple applications are easy to do when you can fill out the Common Application—one application that is accepted by more than 200 schools.

**How Many Applications
Are Enough for Me?**

❑ Have I chosen schools I'd like to call "home" for the next four years?

❑ Will I have enough time, patience, and support at home to get all of my applications out the door by deadline?

❑ Will I regret not filling out longer applications or those that require an essay?

❑ Is my list still long because I'm avoiding making choices?

❑ How much money do I want to spend filing applications?

Different Deadlines

There are four different kinds of deadlines for applications: regular admission, rolling admission, early decision, and early action. Schools may offer the option of more than one kind. Check the deadline requirements for each college you're considering.

Regular and Rolling Admissions

For regular admissions, all applications are reviewed after the submission date deadline, usually in January or February, sometimes in March. The school lets you know in mid-April whether you've been accepted or denied.

In the case of rolling admissions, the school evaluates applications continually as they are received, and lets you know as soon as it has reviewed your application—usually within six weeks. The earlier you apply, the more slots are open. Rolling "admits" are used mainly by large state schools and many less selective schools.

Early Decision and Early Action

The early decision application deadline is mid-October or early November, and the school lets you know—accept, deny, or defer to the regular admissions pool—in mid-December or early January. Decisions are final; if admitted, you agree on your application to go. Some schools do two early decision dates. The more selective schools usually fill one-third or more of the class with this type of admission.

With early decision, the upside is that you find out early and can enjoy the rest of your senior year without the stress of wondering where you are going to college. The downside is that you don't get to compare financial aid offers because the school knows you are coming no matter what the aid package. Also, if your application for early decision is rejected, you'll need to hustle to complete applications to those other schools further down on your list. If it's winter break, you should realize that teachers and counselors won't be available to answer questions or write recommendations.

Recent concerns that early decision policies put too much pressure on applicants and tend to favor financially well-off families have led some highly selective schools to relax their rules, giving students the option of attending other universities, as is the case with early action admissions (see below). One result is that some highly selective schools that have remained rigidly early decision have seen their pool of early applicants drop, creating a greater chance for anyone in the pool to get in. Conversely, those schools that relaxed rules have seen their applicant pool increase, making it more difficult to be admitted early.

In the case of early action, similar to early decision, the school lets you know early—but if you're accepted by the college, you are not bound to go there. Also, you may apply to other schools simultaneously.

One more thing: If either of your parents was an undergraduate at a particular school, you're a legacy and, as such, you may stand a better chance of being admitted than others with fairly equal credentials. If, indeed, a parent's alma mater is your first choice, consider applying early decision. Otherwise, the school might think you're brushing it off.

What Will It Cost to Apply?

Costs vary according to the school and your financial situation. One application can cost $50 or more. The Common Application online does not charge you, but the schools may charge an institutional fee. Fees may be waived for a number of reasons, though, including financial hardship, applying by a deadline set by the college, making your campus visit within certain dates, having alumni parents, or applying to a school that really, really wants you. The bottom line is that you must check with each college about application fees for traditional and Internet submissions.

Completing the Application

One thing is for sure when it comes to filling out college applications: they all take longer than you think, even those requiring only fill-in-the-blanks

Application Due Dates

Admission Type	Application Deadline
Regular	January, February, or March
Rolling	During each school's admission cycle
Early decision	Mid-October or early November
Early action	Mid-October or early November

Five Ways to Get Organized—and Stay That Way

1. Make file folders (for a filing box or on your word processing program) for everything that pertains to the search and applications: ACT/SAT/AP Tests; Activities (High School, Community); Recommendations; Campus Visits; Campus Interviews; Essays; Applications in Progress; and Applications Completed.

2. Keep a master list of where you are applying, which parts of the application are completed, and the mailing deadline.

3. Put deadlines on the refrigerator, mark your calendar, enter on your personal digital assistant—whatever it takes to remind you of impending deadlines for test registration, test taking, picking up recommendations, and filing applications.

4. Ask your parents to lighten up on your household chores while you deal with applications. You can wish they'd cancel chores altogether, but you know that probably won't happen.

5. Recruit a parent to help with the filing and remembering dates—all the logistical things that sap your time.

information such as test scores, classes taken, and possible major. The amount of time it takes to complete more involved applications varies, depending on whether they require one or more essays.

The task is equivalent to at least a part-time job, but one that's crucial to your future. So, you need time to do it right. By being organized and asking for help from parents or guardians, you can make the process smoother and probably do a better job on each application.

Writing Essays

More selective schools require one or more essays. The essay does not have to win a Pulitzer Prize. But it does need to pique the admissions officer's fancy, enough to differentiate you from the thousands of other applicants who also participate in activities and get good grades. The essay is a grand opportunity for you to show your sense of humor, your sense of the world and your place in it, your dreams and goals, your philosophy—whatever makes you tick, which is not just like everyone else.

Does that mean you can get accepted or rejected on the basis of your essay? How much the essay weighs in the admissions decision depends on the particular college. Some colleges simply want to see if you can write sentences with correct grammar and punctuation. Others want, in addition, to see a demonstration of how you think as one indicator of your readiness for college classes and campus life. At some schools your shining essay might be important in a borderline situation. All other things being equal, would you take the student with a boring essay or the one who has a well-articulated point?

You'll find how-to tips for terrific essays in the next chapter.

Recommendations

Recommendations allow admissions officers to get a testimonial about what an asset you would be to that college and why. But good recommendations don't just float from the skies; instead, writing a sparkling recommendation is an art form. Sometimes, even really nice, willing people are unable to write an effective recommendation.

So before asking anyone for a recommendation, you need to figure out three things: (1) which teachers, job supervisors, and community people know you best and like you; (2) which ones have specific anecdotes or experiences with you that will not simply repeat the fill-in-the-blanks information in your application, but amplify your strengths; and (3) which ones are the best writers. People whom you ask to write a recommendation should meet all three criteria and support your aspirations.

How do you figure out which teachers are good writers? Listen to their grammar and vocabulary in class and informally after class, evaluate their handouts, and ask your counselor for suggestions. The school college counselor can probably tell you who writes a lot of recommendations for the kinds of colleges to which you are applying.

If it's Wednesday and you ask people to write recommendations due Friday—bad timing! Give them two weeks. Some teachers even require requests in September because they get so many.

Because teachers may not remember everything you've done once papers have been handed back, give them:

❏ Copies of your outstanding work in their class as a reference

❏ A résumé with activities and honors in school and the community

❏ The college's recommendation form or directions

❏ A stamped, addressed envelope for the completed recommendation

Also, advise the teacher if a college needs specific information. For example, if you're applying to a highly selective college and getting a B instead of an A in math, the teacher still may believe you can succeed at that college. Ask her to discuss why she believes so in the recommendation. Finally, set a time when you'll pick up the recommendation or check on the mailing.

Somewhere in the process, you and your parent may be asked to sign a waiver stating that you will not be able to look at any recommendations. That waiver request can be initiated by the high school, by the person writing a recommendation, or by the college on the application form. Admissions experts suggest that although it's helpful to see your teacher recommendation to know if the teacher has done well by you, you should sign the waiver. Signing demonstrates your confidence that, of course, any recommendation you've requested will be positive.

Generally, you need only teacher and counselor recommendations, unless you have an unusual talent. For instance, if you have studied bagpipes outside of school and play in a band, consider the pipe major or your instructor as an extra recommendation. A yellow caution flag: don't submit more recommendation letters than required unless you're certain the letters are all insightful gems. There's such a thing as overkill.

How I Handled My Letters
of Recommendation

I started working on letters second semester of my junior year. Our [school's] college counselor told me to pick two teachers for recommendations and another person for a character reference. I wanted teachers whom I had known recently. The calculus teacher was probably my best teacher in high school. I went in frequently, so I got to know him well. He cared about what he was doing, which is the most important thing about a teacher. Then I picked my English teacher for similar reasons. We read Emerson and Thoreau; it was some pretty deep stuff. He seemed to really care about helping us learn. I took a lot out of that class. He trusted us. I think that means a lot.

I thought about a couple of my friends' parents and my volleyball coach. I'm captain this year, and it would be good for colleges to see how I interacted on an athletic team. But I decided on the youth director at my church. You could ask her about anything. She helped me become a high school class helper. She knew I liked to work with kids.

My math teacher had this packet I had to fill out for him so he could understand me even more. He asked questions about what I found interesting in class and stuff like what I would be doing in 10 years. New Trier also has a standard recommendation sheet with five questions that students fill out for teachers who'll be writing recommendations. My English teacher used that form.

I asked the youth director for a letter the early part of this [senior] year. I asked my teachers late in my junior year to make sure they had time. They sent the recommendations in their own envelopes, although I did check in with them.

Get the letters out of the way early because lots of teachers scramble to get everything done. Ask teachers you think would know you best, not necessarily where you got the best grades. In many cases, where you can get a good grade, you might not enjoy the teacher or know him or her very well.

Matt Hennessey, New Trier High School, Winnetka, Illinois

FAQ for Online Applications

What's the advantage of an online application?

It saves lots of time and encourages applying to multiple schools. You probably can receive notification of acceptance online rather than waiting for the once-daily USPS delivery.

What's the difference between the online Common Application and a college's online application?

You fill out the Common Application once and can send it to any of the more than 200 colleges that accept it. A college's specific application may not be sent to other schools. However, if any other colleges use the same application service, common data (e.g., name, address, high school attended) will automatically be filled in.

Are online applications free?

Some are; some aren't. The college determines the fee. The fee should be listed on the application. Pay by credit card, as with any other online purchase.

How long does it take to fill out an application?

Without an essay, generally about an hour. Allow time to download any software needed to complete the application.

What about recommendations?

Often, recommendations can be delivered electronically too. If the directions are unclear, check with the admissions office.

How do I know what to do to apply online?

Complete instructions are available with the application. Be sure to save frequently to avoid losing your work.

Your Mistake-Proof Final Checklist

I have:

❑ Spelled all words correctly (check at least once without using spell-check on your computer, plus read printed-out copy of any computer application)

❑ Filled in all the blanks

❑ Answered all the questions

❑ Asked a parent or guardian to proofread the whole application

❑ Included all parts: essay(s), recommendation(s), any required extra materials

❑ Enclosed a signed check or credit card information

❑ Signed and dated all signature lines

❑ Made a copy for my records

About 10 days after sending an application, check with the admissions office to make sure it arrived. If you send applications by regular mail, include a self-addressed, stamped postcard asking the admissions rep to let you know when the packet arrives. And then? Forget about the whole process for a while.

End-of-Chapter Questions

13.1 What kind of organization system should I devise for keeping track of deadlines and the progress of each application? Should I ask parents, guardians, siblings, or mentors for some help with keeping track?

13.2 How many colleges should I apply to? Should I apply to colleges with varying degrees of difficulty for getting in? If my test scores and GPA fit the college's profile, shouldn't I get in?

13.3 What criteria should I use when choosing people to write my recommendations?

13.4 Am I giving myself enough time and paying sufficient attention to neatness and detail so that I don't sabotage my application?

13.5 Do I back up files relating to applications and essays often enough to be adequately protected?

13.6 Have I considered the pros and cons of each type of admission—from regular to early action?

14

10 Ways to Write Your Best Essay Ever

Whether you love it or hate it, the essay on your college application counts toward admission. How much it counts depends on each school. But you don't know how much weight the essay carries and whether it could be the swing factor in your application or for scholarship consideration. So your best bet is to figure out how to write the essay and get to it.

Easier said than done, of course, by someone not writing the essay. Actually, if you are applying to more than one private college, you'll have more than one essay to write. You may be able to tinker and use your first essay for more than one college, but it's unlikely you'll use exactly the same essay. More likely, you'll refashion concepts, thoughts, and paragraphs from the first essay to meet the distinct essay question(s) on other applications.

For example, perhaps one of the most important persons in your life was your grandmother, and College A's essay directive is "Describe a person who influenced you the most." In response you may show through examples how her presence in your life provided direction and strength. Say College B's essay directive is "Describe the greatest challenge you ever faced." You can transfer points you made in the other essay by writing about the realization that, even though your grandmother died recently, her direction and strength continue to serve you.

It's not unusual, though, to write more than one essay from scratch.

Where to Look

A Google search for "college application essays" turned up more than 300,000 sites within a few seconds. The sites offer topic ideas, sample essays, editing, in-depth critiques, and proofreading for fees ranging from about $10 to $600 or more. Be careful of any site that "guarantees" you'll be admitted.

Kinds of Questions

The key to all essays is that they are about you. No matter what the question, the purpose is to give you an opportunity to show the school your values, your curiosity and intellectual growth, characteristics such as your sense of humor, and whether you can articulate your thoughts coherently with correct grammar, sentence structure, and vocabulary. Often those qualities are not recognizable from test scores, class rank, and GPA, the fodder of most state institutions' admissions.

Essay questions generally fall into two categories: personal issues or issues in the world around you. Personal issues questions include your strengths and weaknesses, involvement in extracurricular activities, goals and plans, academic experiences, whom you admire, books you've enjoyed, or personal challenges.

Although the admissions representative wants to know what makes you tick, beware of becoming too familiar by writing about relationship problems or trouble with peers or a particular teacher. If you wouldn't discuss it with your mom or dad, you probably should not write about it in your essay to a total stranger whose job is to evaluate you for admission—or not—to the school.

On the other hand, you may discuss some not-so-good event in your life with an outcome that demonstrates how you have recovered or triumphed. Always accentuate the positive—write more paragraphs on what you've learned and applied to your life rather than the actual event description. Write more about your strengths and show how you turned a weakness or failure into some positive action. You want to be honest, but this is not the time to confess all your foibles. You do want to show what you've learned from any experience and how it has helped shape your long-term goals.

When the question is about a social, cultural, or economic issue, define the issue, discuss options briefly, commit to one option more expansively, and tell why that option appeals to you. Some essay questions might

What about Me?

❑ What activities do I like to do best?

❑ What is it I like to do that most of my friends do not?

❑ How have I challenged myself? Have I had to work particularly hard in a sport, a class, or a nonschool activity? What did I achieve personally? What did I learn about myself?

❑ What kinds of issues do I like to talk about? Politics, war, dishonesty, a school policy, drug or alcohol abuse? What specific example illustrates why I'm interested in a particular issue?

❑ How would I solve a problem or issue in my immediate or larger world?

❑ What three things would I like to accomplish when I am on my own?

ask you to imagine something in the future or discuss the most pressing issue you see today. The key is to narrow the topic, focus on something specific, and use examples to support your opinions. Avoid trying to solve problems that have vexed many governments for decades—you don't have enough essay space.

10 Tips for Writing Great Essays

Regardless of the question, there are some basic tenets for writing essays. Whether you are to write about something personal or a topic relating to pressing issues in today's world, these tips will be helpful.

1. Brainstorm with and without your family. Identify topics about which you feel passionately or enthusiastically—that feeling will come through in your writing. Understand that your parents may feel passionately about a topic that turns you off. Write on the topic of your choice: After all, it is *your* essay.

2. Return to the three points you decided to emphasize when planning campus interviews (Chapter 12). Construct your essay around one or more of those points. That helps build continuity in your application. If one point you want to impress upon the school is your work ethic, you might write about how you began running at age 10 and are still working hard, always trying to improve your personal best time.

3. Choose a topic that differentiates you from the crowd. Consider that Duke University, for example, receives about 16,000 applications for admission each year. To make your essay exceptional, you need to talk about something other than how much you want to go to Duke to play basketball intramurals in Cameron Indoor Stadium.

4. Your essay should have a message—one you can (and should) write down in one sentence on an index card. That helps you focus and not digress from the main topic.

5. Use facts, anecdotes, and experiences that support your point. Including personal insights and ethical beliefs makes the essay yours alone, but the essay must contain more substance than how you feel about an issue or event.

6. Craft a beginning, middle, and end to the essay. Make the tone conversational but delete slang words. The beginning often is a good place for an anecdote or personal experience that sets up the rest of the essay.

7. When you get stuck with writer's block—and every writer does—say out loud what you are thinking, then write down the very words you just spoke. That works amazingly well.

8. Stick to required word length. If instructions say no more than 300 words, that's what the college wants. The admissions representative is not going to count words, but if it takes you 420 words to make your point, edit and cut.

9. When you think the essay is finished, read it out loud to yourself. Check for spelling, phrasing, missing words, and passages that simply don't make sense. Print out your essay and double-check spelling because the spell-check programs do not correct misused words spelled correctly.

10. Ask someone who is a good writer-editor to react honestly to your essay. What does he or she see as the essay message? Does the essay jump around or flow from beginning to end? Did you stay on point or wander? Are sentences too long? Does sentence length vary? Weigh input, then revise and rewrite, probably more than once.

Even though writing about yourself and your opinions might sound like a no-brainer, it takes time and multiple revisions. Even for the most facile writers, writing isn't like opening a box of animal crackers to satisfy a snack-attack. Realistically, double the amount of time you think it will take to write your essay.

How I Put My Essay Together

An admissions officer from Duke talked about one essay that stood out in her mind. It was by a guy in Colorado who went rock climbing all the time. He decided to make his own boots, and his essay went through the whole process and at the end he included a picture of the boots.

So my essay is about an art project that ties in with a job I had the summer before senior year. As part of my job, I gave tours of dorm rooms at Oklahoma City University. Most rooms used simple organizational techniques. I am really into organizing, but I thought you could add a little art flare. I started working on things I'd have to take to college. So the essay explains what I have done for my future dorm room.

I made a rather uninhibited bedside table—a wooden sculpture that looks like metal. I had a lot of fun with a jigsaw. I transferred photographs of my friends onto fabric and sewed a photo-duvet cover. I have that on my bed. I made a room divider out of copper pipes and a reading lamp from the innards of an industrial camp light and the bellows of an antique photo enlarger.

I used the essay on my Common Application, but it will be used on other applications too. Lots of colleges have specific topics, but you can meld your ideas. I'm applying to 11 schools.

First, I always have my mother read any essay; I don't want to take it to my teacher and give her bad work. I want somebody to tell me if it isn't very good, correct the grammar, and make it more like me. If a teacher reads your essay and alters it so much that you think it no longer sounds like you, I'd ask a friend to read it. If she asks "Where did all of 'you' go?" I'd do some more work on the essay. It's important that your essay sound like you.

Work on your essay in advance. I started the summer before senior year with the essay for the common apps.

**Halley Brunsteter, Classen School for Advanced Studies,
Oklahoma City, Oklahoma**

Your Mistake-Proof Checklist

I have:
- ❑ Started every paragraph with a topic sentence
- ❑ Avoided one-sentence paragraphs
- ❑ Put commas in the right places
- ❑ Used complete sentences
- ❑ Checked spelling
- ❑ Stayed within the word limit
- ❑ Printed out a copy to proofread
- ❑ Asked someone else to proofread also
- ❑ Made a copy for my files

End-of-Chapter Questions

14.1 Do all applications require an essay?

14.2 What difference does the essay make to admittance?

14.3 What should I write about? How profound does the essay have to be?

14.4 Who should I ask for input on the essay topic and to critique my essay?

14.5 Can I work with my parents on this or will I be better off seeking help outside the family? Should I use an essay writing service?

14.6 How do I get over writer's block?

14.7 What approach works best for beginning my essay—an anecdote, an example, or a statement of fact or belief?

15

Getting Accepted—or Not

If you thought the search and application process was difficult, try waiting for notification. The drama will ratchet way up at some point between December and April, depending upon which admissions procedure you followed. Check each college's notification dates carefully, since they can differ.

Depending on the school, you will be notified via regular mail or e-mail, which allows you to indicate acceptance and pay your deposit online. Colleges are moving to allow students to check online for the decision rather than wait for official notification.

If accepted, hold your breath until you see the financial aid package, which may not arrive for at least another week. Even if you've been offered a great scholarship package, you still should like the place well

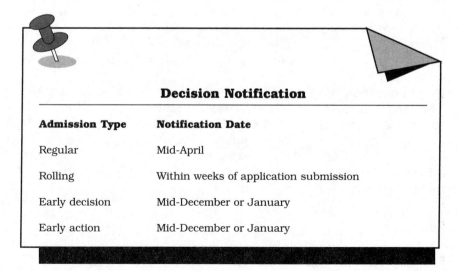

Decision Notification

Admission Type	Notification Date
Regular	Mid-April
Rolling	Within weeks of application submission
Early decision	Mid-December or January
Early action	Mid-December or January

Notification Online

Applicants to Florida State University in Tallahassee can enter a secure site through their specified number (usually Social Security number) and six-digit birth date to find out whether they have been accepted or denied. One parent couldn't wait and typed in the required numbers (with her student's agreement) at midnight when the student was not home.

enough to live there four or, in some instances, five years. Students have been known to say yes to a particular college based solely on scholarship money, then find out the school is wrong for them and end up transferring. Consider again those points that made certain colleges stand out during the search process, why you chose to visit particular campuses, and what you experienced that caused you to apply.

Send thank you notes to colleges that said yes but you rejected. You could end up reapplying there. Also, send thank you notes to people who wrote recommendations for you, telling them which college you've chosen. They're interested or they wouldn't have written the recommendation in the first place.

Admission Denied

Being accepted is easy to take. Being denied admission is hard. If you don't get into a particular school, the rest of your life is not ruined, although the next couple of weeks might be tough. It helps to realize that there is rarely just one perfect college. Rather, there probably are several colleges, similar in nature, and any of them might be a good fit for you.

One big thing you should know is that the denial isn't personal. Most state schools base their decisions on numbers—your GPA and/or standardized test scores. Selective colleges often look for a specific mix of students. Maybe they wanted a percussionist for the orchestra and you play guitar in the jazz band. You can't control the admissions office decision-making process, but you can control how you respond to the decision.

How Am I Dealing with Rejection?

❏ Am I withdrawing from the people who have always supported me? Right now, being with family and friends who have always made me feel positive could be helpful.

❏ Do I feel bitter and angry? Neither emotion tends to move a person forward, if prolonged.

❏ Do I blame others—the admissions officers, my high school counselor or teachers, my parents—for not getting accepted? Have I considered that no one may be to blame?

❏ Am I able to recognize my limitations? Was I realistic about where I applied?

Doing Something Personal about Being Denied Admission

❏ Lie low for a while.

❏ Return to your daily rhythm. Such rhythm has a subtle way of helping people get back on track.

❏ Exercise. Often, the first thing people junk when under stress is exercise, but it is actually good recovery medicine.

Other acceptance/rejection situations probably will occur, too, including:

❏ Friends are accepted where you were rejected.

❏ You are accepted where friends were rejected.

Not Getting into the College of Your Choice

Going to a prestigious college in a city was my whole thing. My dream schools were the University of Chicago and Boston U. On a Monday, I got accepted to BU but didn't get enough scholarship. On Friday, I got wait-listed at Chicago. It was brutal. Both situations came as a huge surprise to me. My credentials were as good as their acceptance rates. In fact, I exceeded their standards. I usually do a good job of grounding myself, but not this time.

First, I cried. Then I got angry. I'm still a little embittered. What helped was talking to people. But I didn't want to hear about how this was part of some greater plan. I hate that. My brother said, "Yeah. You got screwed over and this isn't fair." I needed honesty.

I did have a backup plan—a nice scholarship from the University of Northern Iowa. So I can afford to study overseas, go on spring break, and not have to sell all my stuff. Plus, I'm in the Honors program.

I wish I'd done some things differently. Like kept a more open mind instead of saying, "I want this and this and this." Applied to suburban and smaller schools and schools where I had a better chance for scholarships. Like BU has 30,000 applicants and 30 scholarships! I shouldn't have set myself up as much.

Bridget Gongol, University of Northern Iowa, Cedar Falls

❏ Friends are accepted anywhere and you have not received any notification yet.

❏ You were not accepted at your first-choice school and everyone knows it.

❏ Your parents are disappointed, or you think they are.

Wait-Listing and Deferments

You may be wait-listed by the college, which means neither acceptance nor rejection. The college has accepted a certain number of applicants and is simply waiting to see how many will agree to enroll by the school's required response date, which is usually early May. After that, applicants on

Deferred—and Doing Something about It

I applied for early decision because the acceptance rate is higher for early admission. I must have spent 25 man-hours preparing the application, but didn't know whether I'd get in because of SAT scores. Then I got 33 on the ACT, and Penn takes the higher score so I felt all right. On acceptance day— December 15 at 2 p.m.—I left class during a lecture to log on and found out I was deferred. I was stunned. I'd put so much work into applying that there was really nothing else I could do. I decided what the hell, I'll just call and see if they'll talk about my application.

I was told I was one of many good candidates, which I figured. Then the admissions officer suggested I write a letter saying Penn was still number one and I would come if admitted. He said lots of students hear they are deferred and lose interest.

I sent the letter when I submitted the rest of my applications in January. The afternoon the Penn acceptances came out—April 2 at 4 p.m.—it took half an hour to log on because 15,000 kids were doing that too. Suddenly, this text pops up and says, "Congratulations! You have been accepted to the University of Pennsylvania Class of 2007 as a member of the Wharton School." I memorized that sentence.

Later, we visited Penn and the admissions officer who'd helped me on the phone said my letter was good and that not everyone was as lucky as I about being accepted.

**Boris Shcharansky, Wharton School of Business,
University of Pennsylvania, Philadelphia**

the wait-list are contacted to fill vacant slots. Highly selective schools are usually done with wait-listing by mid-June. Less selective schools may take a little longer since they pick up students who didn't make the cut at the more selective colleges.

Procedures vary according to schools, so you can call the admissions office to ask about the wait-list procedure, where you are on the list, and when notification would be most likely. If you've been wait-listed at your first-choice school, it can't hurt to tell the representative that the school is your first choice and you will come if accepted. In fact, if you don't respond when the college notifies you about being wait-listed, the school may assume you are no longer interested. However, don't flood the admissions office with additional letters of recommendation or information about honors and awards you didn't mention originally.

If you feel uncomfortable, ask your guidance counselor to inquire about your position on the list and put in a good word for you. But discourage your parents or guardians from calling on your behalf. Giving you support at home is their role at this point.

Consider Alternatives

You do have alternatives though. Understandably, it may take a few days to want to consider any of them. You could:

❏ Attend another school that accepted you. You did think it was good enough to send an application to not so long ago.

❏ Enroll in a community college. Good grades there will strengthen any reapplication next year as a transfer student.

❏ Join the armed services.

❏ Wait a year, then apply to college again, when you have a fresh perspective and some new experiences.

Once you start evaluating alternatives using the facts you gather, you'll find your way. But if you still feel overwhelmed and underappreciated, talk with your parents, counselor, a trusted teacher, or an adult friend. Where you go to school won't impact on your future—or your future earnings—as much as what you do while you're at school.

Postponing College

What if everybody you know can barely wait to pack their bags for college, and you're the one senior who wants to jump off the fast-track-to-college train for a year or so? It happens, and for some good reasons: finances, lack of firm education or career goals, study burnout, or just maybe there's a one-time opportunity too good to pass up.

Your family may put forth plenty of good arguments about why you should give college a chance. Your challenges become identifying why you want to postpone college and deciding how you'll spend the time between high school graduation and college. Articulate responses to both challenges are the best way to approach parents who are, at the least, fretting.

Speak with your counselor about waiting a year and doing something constructive, educational, and maybe even exciting. Anything besides pure unbridled fun will probably involve work, paying rent for an apartment or to your parents, and doing your own laundry and meals. Most jobs will be entry-level and low paying. Still, aim for work where you can learn new

Earnings: High School versus College Graduates

Both Sexes/ All Races	High School Graduate	Bachelor's Degree (Including GED)
Ages 25 to 29	$23,980	$39,538
Ages 30 to 34	$25,680	$47,138
Ages 35 to 39	$28,695	$57,185
Ages 40 to 44	$31,284	$59,216
Ages 45 to 49	$32,287	$61,751
Ages 50 to 54	$31,402	$54,914
Ages 55 to 59	$30,522	$58,640

Source: U.S. Census Bureau

skills, mix with people who are different from your friends, and where you have opportunities for advancement, even for noncollege graduates.

Ways to Make the Year (or Longer) Valuable

There are other avenues to consider if going straight to college seems wrong for you right now. Consider whether the choice you make will strengthen another college application down the road. But even more important, consider what you will learn about yourself and how your choice may help determine what you want to do with your life.

Here are some ideas:

❏ If you do end up flipping burgers, you may decide you'd like to run a company, own a business, or be a chef. Whatever you decide, you can use the experiences to strengthen college applications when you decide to go forward.

❏ Volunteer with an organization like Habitat for Humanity. The experience of giving back will change you forever.

❏ Take on a physical challenge such as those offered in Outward Bound. Your self-confidence will soar.

❏ Join the armed forces. You may be able to choose the kind of job you perform in the service, and you'll get training, good benefits, and steady pay while you figure out what to do with your life. The G.I. Bill helps pay for your postservice education too.

❏ Work in AmeriCorps full-time and you'll receive almost $5,000 for college. The type of work varies.

❏ Read a magazine article or book pages every day to help broaden your perspective.

End-of-Chapter Questions

15.1 How do colleges notify students about acceptance or denial? Have I discussed with my parents/guardians which of us has dibs on finding out first?

15.2 Do I understand the financial aid package offered by each school that has accepted me? Which school offers the most scholarship and grant funds that I do not need to repay? Which offers more loans and work study funds?

15.3 What are the pros and cons of each school, and how do they stack up against the aid offered?

15.4 How do I typically handle rejection? Do I blame others or let them help me climb back out of the pits?

15.5 If I get accepted and my best friend doesn't, what should I say? How can I be supportive?

15.6 What's a good backup plan if I don't get into my first-choice school? What makes my first-choice school so appealing? Why is it more appealing than other schools that have similar qualities?

15.7 Have I considered options in case I'm wait-listed or deferred?

15.8 Does putting off college for a while sound good to me? Why? What can I learn, where can I go, what can I do during a year off that will move me forward?

15.9 What's the best way to approach my parents about postponing college?

15.10 Can I earn enough money during the year off to support myself? What kind of help can I expect from my parents?

Part 4

Senioritis and a Very Long Summer

16
Senior Year Attitude

There's just something about senior year of high school. Maybe it's in the water, because "senioritis" is a recognized state by students, parents, and educators throughout the country. Adults view it one way, students another. For example, adults say their youngsters get extra squirrelly. They may suffer from any combination of inattentiveness, spaciness, moodiness, and lack of enthusiasm about schoolwork, activities, and family. Also, says Peter Pashler, a parent of two boys, "There's a certain arrogance—the rules don't apply to me anymore."

Students, on the other hand, say parents won't let up or let go. The parents still want to know with whom and where the youngsters go after school and dinner, what's for homework, and when tests are scheduled. They expect seniors to still have curfews, often including the summer before college. One wag has suggested that all this senior year tension is intended to make parents so relieved their children are going to college that they won't miss them so much when they leave home.

Classes and Grades Still Matter

The consequences of taking it easy first semester, second semester, or both during senior year can be serious. Colleges frown on it, and your senioritis may affect their admission decisions. When admission is not based solely on test scores and/or GPA, colleges carefully look at your senior year course load to see how you have challenged yourself. It's likely you'll need to list classes, which ideally include Honors or AP classes. Colleges may require a midyear grade report from your counselor as part of your application record. If you're taking the easy route, you show you are not quite

Do I Have a Bad Case of Senioritis?

You betcha, if you answer yes to even half of these statements:

- ❑ I load up on easy classes and study halls.
- ❑ I blow off homework assignments as nonessential.
- ❑ I don't have time for extracurricular clubs—they're too stupid.
- ❑ School is driving me crazy—why can't it just be over?
- ❑ I can't stand to be around home.
- ❑ My parents are completely out-of-touch with what I think and want.
- ❑ Let someone else walk the dog every day.
- ❑ Curfews? I don't need curfews.
- ❑ Party? I love to party. I can sleep in school.

How I Stayed Focused on School My Senior Year

I was either in classes I was extremely interested in or that didn't require a whole lot of work. A required class that didn't require much work was government, which you can take as an AP or regular class. I took regular because I didn't need the AP credit and am not interested in government, so I could do the little assignments needed and not spend a whole lot of time on it. But I loved biology—I absolutely love biology—and had hours and hours of homework at night, but I was so interested I would read parts of the book before they were due in class.

I took seven classes plus an independent study: AP biology, AP language and composition, AP Spanish, band, choir, government, probability and statistics, and an independent study for a religion credit. I did about four to five hours homework a night, but the AP classes made it all worth it.

My counselor discouraged me from taking so much when I had to sign up my junior year [for senior year classes]. But I wanted to do biology, which I didn't need, and I felt committed to the band and choir groups after participating for three years, and religion was my own independent study.

Kelly Fitzpatrick, University of St. Thomas, St. Paul, Minnesota

ready for prime college time, either intellectually or in terms of maturity. You may argue that regardless of senior class choices, you are strong college material, but colleges will put more weight on your senior year record.

Senioritis also can strike after you have been admitted to one or more colleges. Most colleges will have a caveat in the acceptance letter such as, "Your admission is contingent on your continued successful performance." They may withdraw your admission or scholarship offer if grades drop significantly. Kelly Fitzpatrick's scholarship awards from the University of Saint Thomas in St. Paul, Minnesota, were not credited to her tuition bill until midsummer after the school received her final grades. If grades have suffered because of a change in your circumstances, such as parental divorce, change of custody arrangements, or serious illness for you or a family member, call or write to the college, because that is not a reflection of senioritis.

Of course, not all students slack off noticeably senior year, despite their eagerness to move on from high school. If you have taken appropriate classes, honed study and time management skills through balancing schoolwork, activities, and, perhaps, a job, you are more likely to sustain your record during the senior year.

Who's in Charge?

Regardless of how much—or how little—senioritis you feel, senior year and its companion summer signal changes in rules on the home front. Should parents give up all control? Absolutely not, says Rich Kelly, a parent of five. He says parents can't be friends with their children until they are fully adults. That means the Kelly household does not run on democratic principles, and everyone follows family rules. Some parents are akin to "benevolent dictators"—they listen, discuss options, allow or agree to some different rules, but reserve their right to the final decision on all things affecting the youngsters and household. Other parents, though, do give up control. Obviously, the one-size-fits-all rule does not apply to families.

Regardless of how family rules are (or are not) set, discussions may not always be calm. Look for ways to ease rules rather than toss them out completely, and strive for compromise. For instance, if your friends have later curfews or none at all, ask your parents if you can have everybody over to your house to watch DVDs for the night. If you want to go to the beach on Saturday but your folks want you to visit Aunt Emma with them, suggest that you and Aunt Emma have dinner alone some evening next week.

When you and your parents are at odds about how to handle a particular situation, brainstorming options can go a long way toward avoiding conflict. Senior year and summer allow many opportunities for you to test your decision-making skills while parents are still around as a safety net. (Not surprisingly, parents will find out about some of your decisions only when you are thirtysomething and telling stories.)

What Rules Do I Still Need to Follow?

- ❑ Do the rules help me reach my educational or career goals?
- ❑ Are the rules intended to treat all family members fairly? Do they promote family harmony?
- ❑ Do the rules help me show respect for my parents, siblings, friends, teachers, and community?
- ❑ Do the rules mean I take responsibility for my actions and accept the consequences?

Reaching a Mutual Agreement with My Parents about Rules

Things started getting worse in the middle of high school, when you're finding out about everything. But it got worse after my senior year basketball season ended because that meant I could go out later and hang out with my friends. The big fight was about staying over with a friend after graduation parties, and I got my way. After that, it was not as big a deal because I wasn't in high school anymore. I always told my parents where I was going and that I'd be home around a certain time because then they trusted me more. And I'd wake them when I got home.

Also, I got yelled at because I was always on the go and didn't do any work around the house. That's when I realized I actually was always on the go. So I started waking up earlier and asking if I could do anything, and knew I could go out that night.

The worst actually was when I came back from college for my first visit home. I got yelled at because I was out late. I asked, "What do you think I do when I'm away at school?" I think my mom understood because next day there was nothing wrong. But you know, I really don't know what parents think.

You can't judge what's right or wrong in your family by other people's lives. It's as hard for parents as it is for us. And you aren't the only one going through a change.

Sally Scharr, University of Wisconsin-Platteville

Five Ways to Beat Senioritis

1. Schedule a hands-on class in something you are curious about. (That's in addition to four core courses.) Fun projects help maintain interest in school.

2. Build in a specific exercise time at least three days a week—bicycling, jogging, jazz dancing, or any combination of exercise activities.

3. Temporarily avoid friends with serious senioritis.

4. Take a cool-down time-out on your own just before you want to blow up at a parent or sibling.

5. Talk to a school counselor or favorite teacher if you feel at odds with your world as it is.

End-of-Chapter Questions

16.1 What is "senioritis"? Is it a medical malady? Is it the same in Arkansas as Maine?

16.2 Do my senior year grades and classes count for college admissions? Why do colleges care about senior year performance?

16.3 What happens if my final semester senior grades are much lower than other years? How will the college know?

16.4 If there are circumstances beyond my control regarding grades, should I tell the colleges to which I am applying? Am I being realistic about those circumstances or using them as an excuse?

16.5 Does everyone else I know seem to have senioritis? If I don't have senioritis, will I still have fun with my group of friends?

16.6 Why would I need to have a curfew at home when I'm old enough to join the Army?

16.7 Do I make a conscious effort to understand my parents' point of view or, at least, to aim for some sort of harmony on contentious issues?

16.8 Am I willing to compromise? How about my parents being willing to compromise? Is this something we can discuss?

16.9 When disagreements arise, do my parents and I consider several options to solve the problem?

17
Orientation

All of a sudden your boxes and clothes are stuffed in your residence hall room, your parents are leaving, and you don't have a best friend with whom to face the hundreds of new people you'll meet in the next hours and days. No wonder students going to orientation often have mixed emotions—they're finally free, independent, and on their own, but now it seems a tad lonely out there.

Schools fill that gap pretty quickly with myriad activities to make the transition to college as seamless as possible. The school recognizes you have new responsibilities—choosing courses, managing money, establishing a sense of community—and brings together resources to master them. That's because research shows that students who have a good freshman orientation experience are more likely to be successful socially and academically and to graduate, which after all is the ultimate purpose of the whole get-into-college process.

Orientation, usually mandatory, occurs at different times from June through September, depending on the school. Large universities are likely to hold orientation earlier in the summer for choosing classes and hearing about rules and policies. Students do not move in, though they may be able to see their room, or at least their residence hall.

Before the fall semester, freshmen gather again to explore social and service options and get answers to any academic questions. This time they move in too. Smaller schools are likely to hold the entire orientation just before the fall semester begins. The cost is free, minimal, or already incorporated into student fees, such as the deposit that was sent when you accepted the school's invitation to matriculate.

Orientation lasts anywhere from a couple days to a week and is crammed full of social and academic activities. Orientation calendars are often available online, but you'll receive a more detailed packet in the

Orientation on the Appalachian Trail

One of the main reasons I chose Williams was because of its accessibility to the outdoors. The wilderness orientation trip at the beginning of freshman year quickly affirmed my decision to come here and was the unofficial start of my love affair with Williams.

My WOOLF [Williams Outdoor Orientation for Living as a First-year] group—nine first-years and two sophomore leaders—spent five days backpacking 42 miles on the Appalachian Trail. Our trip was for experienced hikers, but WOOLF also has beginner and intermediate trips that don't trek as far. Also, first-years could choose rock climbing or canoe trip options. You provide personal clothing, but WOC [Williams Outing Club] provides food, tarps for shelters, group gear, and whatever personal equipment people don't own. Obviously, some people who haven't been backpacking before feel a bit anxious about whether they'll be able to carry the pack or freeze to death. But the trained leaders help ease the anxiety and people generally get comfortable pretty fast.

Although we were a bunch of strangers, the trip was an awesome group bonding experience. There's usually an unofficial competition among groups to finish the enormous quantities of food WOOLF provides. My trip consumed everything, right down to the spices in Ziploc bags. By the end, people were squirting mustard down their throats. If that's not a bonding experience, I don't know what is.

It can sometimes be tough to make close friends your first semester. But before regular orientation even started, I was already close to my co-WOOLFies, and my leaders became some of my most valued informal advisors during college. In fact, our WOOLF trip has had several reunions.

The post-WOOLF orientation was mostly concerned with the logistics of college: learning the rules, trying not to get lost, picking classes, and checking out the girls. Orientation wasn't bad, but WOOLF was an awesome introduction to Williams.

Zach Yeskel, Williams College, Williamstown, Massachusetts

How to Say Hello to Strangers

❑ Right off the bat, realize that millions of people are shy—not just you.

❑ Silence often makes other people uncomfortable. Always have something meaningful in mind to say when meeting a stranger.

❑ Look the stranger in the eye. That says, "Hey, I'm happy to meet you." And if the two of you shake hands, don't let your arm seem like a wet noodle.

❑ Open the conversation by telling the stranger you are happy to meet him or her. That puts a pleasant, positive spin on the situation right away.

❑ Refer to what's going on around you so both of you find common ground immediately. If you're on a preorientation kayaking trip, for instance, say, "I've never kayaked before. Have you?"

❑ Turn attention onto the stranger with a question: "How did you come to choose this college?" Or a comment: "I wonder if I'll ever find space in my room for all the stuff I brought!"

❑ Think about what the stranger is saying to you rather than what you might respond. If you're really listening to the other person, you're not thinking of yourself.

❑ If shyness is a deep-seated problem, consider seeking professional help. About 5 million Americans have some form of social anxiety disorder or social phobia.

mail. Regardless of how cheesy the activities sound, join in—it's the fastest way to meet a lot of classmates, upperclassmen, professors, and administrators. You've got to meet them sometime, and the easiest way is when all freshmen are equally befuddled.

Social Activities

Social events that begin during orientation will probably extend to the early part of the semester: dances, comedy shows, fireworks, games at the rec center, ice cream socials, fraternity and sorority rush, and downtown street festivals for off-campus exploration. You'll also have opportunities to learn about student organizations and community service. Best bet: Join at least one organization to meet people and give structure to your weeks. Of course, if you join 10, you'll never have time to sleep, much less study.

Many schools offer either optional or required participation in group activities organized around a special interest. It's a terrific way to get to know someone to sit with at the dining hall the first week. At Williams College in Williamstown, Massachusetts, almost 65 percent of the class of 2007 participated in the Williams Outing Club's four-day, three-night wilderness trips. Other students chose between activities geared toward community service and getting to know cultural options or exploring visual arts and dance. As part of orientation, participation is free.

Academic Activities

As much as the schools encourage you to have a life with activities and friends, they also expect you've arrived on campus to learn and prepare for a career. And you can't do that without going to class. So academic information is a key component of the orientation schedule. Generally, you'll hear about academic programs, degree requirements, how to build your class schedule, academic support, and other campus resources. There will be a campus tour, placement tests (foreign language and math) to determine your appropriate course level, and a meeting with an academic advisor. Finally, you'll register for classes.

Students often are divided into small groups to foster questions and meet classmates. You'll get information on residence hall life ranging from rules and food service to packing tips. Some schools hold discussions, resembling seminars, of preassigned readings, indicating the kind of intellectual stimulation the school fosters while allaying some of the first-day-in-class anxieties.

Register for Classes

Freshman class registration occurs during orientation. Most schools have only online registration. You will either receive the fall-spring class options in the mail or access them online.

Despite that long list of exciting classes, freshmen soon realize they don't have all that many choices. They must take required core curriculum courses and prerequisites for a major (if they know it). The crunch comes when sophomores, juniors, and even seniors compete for some of the same classes, ones they skipped as freshmen because either the class was filled or they wanted to explore other subjects. Also, students are vying for the best times: How many students do you know who desperately want an 8 a.m. class five days a week?

What Classes Should I Take?

1. Do I know what I want to major in? Or, do I have a few possibilities in mind?

2. What prerequisite classes are listed for majors of interest to me?

3. How many credits do I need to graduate in four years? Five years? How many credits must I take each semester?

4. In addition to required freshman classes, have I marked some that simply sound interesting?

Tips for Creating a Good Schedule

❏ Try to allow blocks of study time each day.

❏ Give yourself time to eat a healthy breakfast and lunch.

❏ Create a balance by scheduling a less challenging class along with a more demanding one.

❏ Spread out over several semesters the more difficult classes and labs to help yourself meet any GPA requirements for scholarships you've been awarded.

❏ Check the final exam schedule to make sure you're not taking two or three finals the same day.

❏ Ask upperclassmen about professors' teaching styles because they are not all great teachers; some are better researchers.

❏ While some adjuncts (part-time) and/or first-year teachers may be excellent, many may not have fully figured out the workload or their grading system. Generally, it's best to avoid their classes.

Must-Know Procedures

Amid all the orientation information will be major-league important handouts on the school's policies and procedures. Those handouts are more than wallpaper material. They are the key to helping you out of messes before you get into any.

How to Register Online

Sign up as soon as allowed for the best chance of getting classes you want when you want them. From your school's Web site, select "Current Students" and click menu items leading to online registration and class schedule. You will see detailed directions for how to register online. Some basics:

❑ Read all instructions and rules before signing on to register. You may want to print out the instructions for quick reference once you begin your enrollment time.

❑ Know your student identification number and security number assigned by the school. Do not share these numbers with anyone.

❑ Figure your schedule before logging on to sign up for classes because many schools have time restrictions. Michigan State University in East Lansing, for example, limits registration time to 30 minutes per single session, five times per day, and three invalid log-on attempts per session.

❑ Know the number of credit hours you want to sign up for. Michigan State's computer automatically blocks scheduling more than 20 credits except with your academic advisor's permission, which you must get ahead of time.

❑ Enroll as early as possible at your directed time. Be prepared to not gain access immediately because other students are seeking similar access.

Take, for example, the handout that gives dates for class drop-and-adds. If you sign up for a calculus or ceramics class that turns out to be the class from hell and you want out, you must get the proper drop form signed by the appropriate professor or advisor and give it to the correct administrative office *on time*. If you miss the drop date, you will receive a grade based on your efforts regardless of whether you ever step foot in the class again. Saying you didn't know about the drop date won't erase the bad grade.

You and your parents will receive the school's written policy about topics including bills and grade reports, cheating, plagiarism, hate crimes, inappropriate Internet use, violation of residence hall alcohol or drug policy, as well as nonacademic events such as arrests or medical problems. Most schools require you to sign waivers allowing your parents to receive information about your academic performance, medical issues, and disciplinary actions on or off campus. Some schools notify parents in the event of a medical emergency resulting from self-destructive behavior. Also, schools may notify parents of sanctions for violation of residence hall drug and alcohol rules. You and your parents must be aware of the school's disclosure policies and sign whatever waivers suit your situation with the appropriate offices during orientation.

If Not-So-Good Stuff Happens

Colleges and universities want you to participate in school functions, use school facilities, feel safe, live in a safe environment, and be able to express yourself freely. To that end, schools have systems in place to handle minor or major not-so-good events in your life.

If you are a victim of theft, accused of a crime, or in need of counseling for any reason ranging from test stress to sexual assault, you should learn during orientation how the university will respond. You should be given

Campus Resources for Help

All campuses do not have the same resources. The list below notes advocacy and protective services you should inquire about at orientation. (Some people suggest inquiring about these resources during your campus visit and before you commit to the school.)

- ❏ Campus security: Available 24 hours a day, the department should have patrols and safe-ride transportation. It may also have programs such as self-defense clinics and theft prevention. Crime statistics for the university and the surrounding area should be readily available on request.
- ❏ Options for reporting assault or abuse
- ❏ Counseling resources via phone, drop-in, and/or appointment
- ❏ Sexual abuse crisis and resource line
- ❏ Lesbian, gay, bisexual, and transgender resource line
- ❏ Tenant/landlord association
- ❏ Formal groups for Latinos, African Americans, women, and others
- ❏ Student legal services
- ❏ Student medical services
- ❏ Phone numbers for key administrators, such as the dean of students, vice president for student services, and/or dean of freshman students

a list of advocacy and protective services and contact information. Tuck it in an accessible place and call one of those numbers for help or referral. Also, your parents should receive the same information.

Parent Orientation

Parents and families or guardians are likely to have a concurrent orientation program separate from yours. The aim is to help parents understand college life and what you, their student, can expect, so they still feel connected but can cut the cord. Still, baby boomer parents are generally used to intense involvement in their youngsters' education and activities, and some remain active participants. At West Virginia University in Morgantown, for example, parents prevailed on the school to start a shuttle to Pittsburgh International Airport.

Universities, though, are not set up to maintain that strong parental involvement, says Andrew Cinoman, director of Orientation Services at the University of Iowa. Instead, Iowa works to make parents feel connected through understanding the school's facilities, services, academic opportunities, and how parents can assist their students in the transition to college. "Parents can brainstorm with their students, but for the students' development, the students need to handle problems," Cinoman says. "Classroom and course issues, working with an advisor to determine a major, or medical issues—students themselves need to address such issues to mature."

Parents also hear about dealing with homesickness—yours and theirs— and adjusting to the different person who probably will come home at Thanksgiving. That's because college is an environment where students grow, change, modify, explore, discover, challenge, and embrace new ideas and people. It's really not so different from when they left that kindergartener 13 years ago. Except you're a lot taller now.

End-of-Chapter Questions

17.1 Is orientation required? How long will it last? When is it?

17.2 Do my parents come too? Why should they come along? Will they be with me the whole time?

17.3 How can I prepare myself for days of meeting a whole, huge community of new people?

17.4 When can I move into my residence hall?

17.5 How do I find out about organizations to join?

17.6 What considerations must I weigh before registering for first-semester classes? Where do I go if I have questions about registering?

17.7 What classes do I have to take? What classes do I want to take? How can I best mix the two? In addition to my parents, where else can I go to get advice on classes to take?

17.8 Besides course load, what other factors should I consider in class selection?

17.9 Do I understand the school policy for dropping and adding classes? Is there any wiggle room within those rules?

18
Roommate Choices

Almost every freshman has a roommate, or two, three, even four. You may get the roommate who cracks knuckles, the one who thinks showers are a waste of good water, or the almost perfect one who acts and thinks just like you. Until you know, there's bound to be some anxiety mixed with anticipation concerning the kind of roommates you'll have.

The roommate questionnaire that accompanies the college's acceptance congratulations and packet is an attempt to match you with compatible roommates. Although some roommates swear that housing officials picked names out of a barrel, officials generally try to consider student behaviors and choices, knowing roommate adjustment can be trying.

The questionnaire will ask about your living habits. Are you a neatfreak or does the floor become your dresser and dirty clothes depository? Do you smoke? Drink alcoholic beverages? Have religious, ethnic, racial, or sexual preferences? Do you have a physical or learning handicap requiring specific housing options? Prefer coed or single gender halls? Study halls? Honors halls? Other specific interest halls? You need to be truthful on your questionnaire. Your parents should respect your privacy if you prefer not to discuss or show them your completed form.

You can ease first-meeting jitters by contacting your roommate before you arrive at the college. (Most colleges send you the roommate's name during the summer.) E-mail makes it easy to connect, and you will at least know one person on your hall when you arrive. For some, that's comforting.

Another reason to contact that roommate/stranger is to figure out who is bringing what for your common oasis. That prevents having two refrigerators, two TVs, and no space for computers. You can discuss room layout, colors you like for bedspreads and rugs, favorite posters. But what if one roommate insists on taking her drafting table, and the other room-

Who Is My Ideal Roommate?

❏ Do I want to room with someone who thinks just like me?

❏ Would I be comfortable living with someone with a different background?

❏ How do I feel about living with someone with strict religious beliefs? Or if I have strong religious beliefs, do I want to be paired with an atheist or agnostic?

❏ How flexible am I? Can I sleep with my roomie's study light on until 2 a.m.? Do I need to hear my roommate's bluegrass music obsession all the time?

❏ What personal habits of my friends drive me crazy? Nail biting? Gum cracking? Finger tapping? Could I live with someone who has any of those habits—or all of them?

❏ How much privacy do I want for entertaining friends? Or when my roommate has friends in the room?

The Pros of Rooming with High School Friends

❏ I feel more secure rooming with someone I already know.

❏ I won't have to worry about whether we'll like each other.

❏ We'll meet other people in our classes and the organizations we join.

mate, a voracious reader, wants megabookcases for a postage-stamp-size room? Parents report mixed reactions from their students when they put in their two cents' worth—this is pretty much the students' gig.

Despite summer e-mails and phone calls, Rachel Lenz and her Vassar roommate had to punt when they arrived and discovered that the room was smaller than they'd expected (not an uncommon event). That November, they rearranged their room so each had one side, which provided some private space rather than all of it shared, to their mutual delight.

The Cons of Rooming with High School Friends

❏ That loud laugh was okay in high school when I went out in groups, but now it's in my room, all the time.

❏ I didn't know my friend was such a slob/neat-freak/snorer.

❏ I won't meet as many people as I would if I had to be totally on my own.

Rooming with My High School Friend Didn't Work at All

My roommate and I had been inseparable by high school senior year. Because of her, I wanted to go to Ball State. But before college began, I had doubts. We had different ways of solving conflicts. I came from a family that doesn't yell; hers yelled. Also, she'd stay up until 4 a.m. with the light on and the stereo on; I'm a light sleeper.

Other girls living with high school friends were having problems too. By second semester I didn't even want to be in the room with her. Because of our problems, I was going home a lot on weekends and didn't want to come back to Ball State. Finally, the RA [resident assistant] got involved and my roommate moved out before spring break. We'd spent the summer before school buying everything and splitting the cost, so in the end we had to split things up, kind of like when people get a divorce.

Some people are wonderful friends but don't always make wonderful roommates. We decided the only way to save the friendship was for one of us to move out. Neither of us had lived with someone before. When there's pressure, you take things out on your family. At school, your roommate is your family. Unfortunately, we were unable to repair our friendship even after she moved out. So I didn't just lose a roommate, I lost a friend.

Chrisy Muhler, Ball State University, Muncie, Indiana

Rooming with My High School Friend Worked Just Fine

I met Brad in second grade and we went through high school together. He decided to study aviation at Purdue; I wanted landscape architecture, and Purdue was my only choice. When we both got accepted, we decided to room together. We'd heard it didn't always work out, but usually the people we heard it from were girls. I had guy friends in high school who would get mad at each other and yell at each other, but then they were over it. Girls seem to hold grudges a long time.

Once school started, we didn't see each other that much and never had classes together. We saw each other around six, and in the evenings just hung out. I'm sure if we had spent whole days together—like a Saturday—there might have been quarrels. But we'd venture off by ourselves to get away. You can get too much of somebody.

When the school picks your roommate, you can end up with someone you aren't going to like right from the beginning. But I'd also say be careful about rooming with a friend you haven't known very long. You find out a lot about another person really quickly. Brad and I knew each other for so long that we knew everything we were getting into.

He transferred to aviation school before sophomore year and I definitely missed him. I joined a fraternity to fill the space.

Kyle Baugh, Purdue University, West Lafayette, Indiana

Oops, We're Not Alike at All

What happens if you can't stand your roommate after the first two weeks? He flaunts his unlimited funds; you had to earn scholarships to come here. She has never shared a room and doesn't like it now; you shared your room with your sister and were looking forward to having somebody else around. The two of you have nothing in common and even less to talk about.

If you have to, you can figure out another place to study, eat with other people, and still be civil. Needless to say, you'll be looking for compatible friends to live with next semester or next year.

When to Request a Change

It's not unusual for roommates to have conflicts. They live in close, some-times cramped quarters. Some schools house freshmen in triples or quads. Officials tend to let roommates work out their problems, figuring they will benefit from the experience. Generally, parents should not get involved in roommate conflicts except as listeners when you vent.

What about the nightmare roommate, though? The one whose favorite reading is hard porn, has room parties often and late, or has sex with a

Changing Roommates at the End of First Semester

I went from a graduating class of 19 to UND's 13,000 students. The transition in size wasn't so big a deal. The real issue was my roommate. Her sister was a UND student and lived in an apartment, so my roommate was always over there. She wouldn't come back until later at night and then she wasn't always that quiet. The stress of living in a two-by-four room became more stressful. We never got to know each other very well. I'm really shy and it's hard to take off and meet people on my own. I thought I would have her, so I could go with at least one other person. I knew who other people were, but everybody already had their groups. I had nothing to do on weekends so I always went home. Emotionally, I was breaking down.

At the end of first semester you can talk to your RA about changing roommates. My chemistry lab partner's roommate dropped out of school so I moved in with her. That's when things went a lot better. As far as hard feelings when I told my first roommate I was moving out—there were none. We both understood where I was coming from. But now, when we pass each other on campus, we just nod.

I'd say, especially for kids who are shy, go to every activity your dorm floor puts on. You always have a chance of meeting people there. Try to get to know your roommate right away. If there are problems, sit down and try to talk about them. Don't be miserable for a whole semester. If it doesn't work, see about finding a different roommate. When I kept going home, I was allowing myself to not meet anybody. I was avoiding the whole situation.

Tera Field, University of North Dakota, Grand Forks

partner while you're studying 10 feet away at your desk with your earphones on. Don't panic. You do have options and should pursue them.

First discuss the situation with your roommate. If that gets you nowhere fast, go to the residence hall assistant, or if necessary, the resident hall director. If the roommate's behaviors warrant disciplinary action, the RA will take it from there. If the behaviors aren't against the rules, the RA should discuss the situation with you and your roommate. You still can request a transfer to a different room.

If, however, your roommate threatens you, hits you, or has a weapon in violation of school policy, you need to go immediately to the RA or other authority. If you tell your parents—and you should—a parent should also call the school at once. At orientation your parents should have been given a list of phone numbers for school officials and told who to call for various problems or emergencies.

End-of-Chapter Questions

18.1 How will I tell the college my preferences for housing and a roommate?

18.2 How honest should I be in answering the questions? If I don't want to share space with a person who isn't the same religion, will the school think I'm biased and take back the letter of acceptance?

18.3 What are the advantages and disadvantages of rooming with my high school friend?

18.4 What should I do if I don't like my roommate? Or my roommate thinks I'm a nerd or geek?

18.5 When should I discuss roommate situations with the RA?

18.6 What should I do if my roommate threatens me?

18.7 How involved should my parents be if my roommate situation is bad?

19

Should You Join a Fraternity or Sorority?

A common question for students heading to college is whether they should "go Greek." If the answer is yes, they will aim to join fraternities and sororities, social organizations that also perform educational and philanthropic missions. Each organization bears a Greek letter name and may be a local fraternity or a chapter of a national fraternity. A chapter may have a large house; houses usually are grouped in an area or line a street. Greeks also may live as a group in a residence hall section or individually among the non-Greeks, who are called "Independents."

Reasons Pro and Con

Not all schools have fraternities and sororities, though they may have other sorts of clubs that fulfill similar social functions. Greek pervasiveness and influence varies from campus to campus. About 24 percent of the 29,000 University of Illinois at Urbana-Champaign undergraduates are in the Greek system. There are 53 fraternities and 32 sororities. On the other end, about 1 percent of the 15,000 undergrads at the University of Alaska-Anchorage have gone Greek, an addition to campus life since 1997. Tom Tronick, associate dean of students at Drake University in Des Moines, Iowa, says about one-third of the students are Greeks; Independents have good friends who are Greeks, and Greeks have good friends who are Independents.

Proponents note that the Greek system provides you with an instant community when you join; you'll learn social skills, time management, and practice leadership, all of which are important when you graduate into the work

Greek Vocabulary

Greek: applies to all sororities and fraternities

Fraternity: formally applies to men's and women's organizations; informally refers only to men's groups

Sorority: women's organizations

Chapter: local group of the national organization

Rush: recruitment; the process by which individuals get to know members of particular houses and vice versa

Invitational party: admission by invitation only; issued after people have gone through Rush

Bid: a formal written invitation to join a chapter

Active: an initiated undergraduate member

Legacy: a person whose mother/father, sister/brother, or grandmother/grandfather was a member of that chapter

world. Additionally, houses adopt philanthropic causes, enabling members to give back to the community. Another factor Drake University has noted over the last 10 years, says Tronick, is student retention, which is higher for students in the fraternity system. "They seem to be more social, which affects their grades slightly, but they are more persistent in getting the degree," he says.

Detractors say affiliation is expensive when you total dues, special collections, projects, and perhaps extra fees for remodeling the fraternity or sorority house. Further, a house at times may require participation, strongly suggest appropriate attire for events, and be homogeneous in terms of ethnicity, economics, and interests. Alcohol consumption and abuse by Greeks has been an ongoing issue, and many schools have barred on-campus parties and instituted campuswide educational programs.

Freshman and sophomore or transfer students evaluating the fraternity system at a particular campus should utilize the informal grapevine and ask around about individual houses. You can also check with the dean of students about houses that may be on probation, have incurred other disciplinary action, or have won campus or community awards.

Rush

The only way to join a fraternity or sorority is to go through Rush, a series of social events that lasts about a week, depending on the size of the Greek community. Rush may occur before or during the fall semester or at the beginning of spring semester. The process is simple: you sign up, attend Greek house parties, and decide which houses you'd like to revisit to meet more members and get to know the house better. Simultaneously, the Greek houses are evaluating you and other prospective members and designating whom they would like to invite back.

Disappointment occurs when house preferences don't overlap with yours and you don't receive invitations to some of your favorite houses. Indeed, some students may potentially receive no return invitations. At the end of Rush, houses issue bids to those who they want to become

Research before You Rush

❑ **www.nicindy.org/index.html** is the Web site for the North American Interfraternity Conference, which represents 66 men's fraternities with members on more than 800 campuses. The site has information specifically for parents as well as general information about recruitment, benefits, and expectations for members.

❑ **www.npcwomen.org** is the site for the National Panhellenic Conference, an umbrella organization for 26 international and national women's fraternities and sororities, with members on more than 620 college campuses in the United States and Canada. The site lists links to many organizations with general information as well as information for those who have questions on specific issues such as eating disorders, alcohol, and other drugs.

❑ **www.nalfo.org** is the site for the National Association of Latino Fraternal Organizations, an umbrella organization established in 1998 for Latino Greek organizations. NALFO has 24 member organizations in the United States.

❑ **www.nphchq.org/home.htm** is the site for the National Pan-Hellenic Council. Established in 1930 at Howard University, it is composed of nine African American international Greek letter sororities and fraternities with a strong service commitment.

members. If you accept, you become a pledge and enter a probationary period during which you and the house members get to know each other.

Hazing

Pledges have requirements to meet, but enduring hazing should not be one of them. Hazing is when pledges are subjected to abusive tricks or ridicule. It can take many forms—such as demanding alcohol ingestion, staying on one's knees for hours, or being left blindfolded somewhere at night. Although hazing is virtually impossible to eradicate everywhere, many states have outlawed it, and institutions' conduct policies often forbid it. You and your parents should know you have remedies, including reporting actions to the college and police.

"[Any] activity that puts one at risk of death or serious bodily injury, such as forcing someone to drink 21 shots of alcohol, can generally be prosecuted criminally," writes Joel Epstein in *Sex, Drugs, and Flunking Out*. Epstein is the former director of special projects and senior attorney for the U.S. Department of Education's Higher Education Center for Alcohol and Other Drug Prevention.

Should I Go Greek?

❑ Do I make friends fairly easily?

❑ Do I prefer one group of friends or do I have friends from scattered groups or interests? If I go Greek, will I still have time for friends in those other groups?

❑ Is the size of the school I've chosen intimidating? Will I feel like I'm a number if I stay Independent?

❑ Will I find others with similar interests through campus organizations?

❑ Will I be able to develop leadership skills and better my social skills or comfort level by joining a fraternity or sorority or by becoming a member of one or more campus organizations?

❑ Do Greek members fill the majority of leadership positions in non-Greek organizations?

❑ Do Independents organize social, cultural, and intellectual events regularly?

❑ Do Independents in residence halls stay on campus on weekends?

Staying Independent and Loving It

Rush is during Welcome Week, the week before school begins. I signed up to do Rush at orientation earlier in the summer because the Greek system advertises then and the Rush fee is cheaper—$30 then and $40 during Welcome Week.

You have to visit all the sororities. You visit 12 houses the first day. Then you narrow your choices to 8, the sororities narrow their choices too, and you go back to choices that have overlapped. Then 4 houses, then 2, and the last day you know which one you are in.

One thing that's really cool is the sorority houses are really beautiful. One was originally the chancellor's house; some have incredible views of the San Francisco Bay and bridge. If you want the nicest housing at Berkeley, join a sorority. Some require you to live there; most do not. None expect you to live there until your sophomore year.

I was surprised about the time requirements. Every Monday you must spend most of your nonclass time at the sorority house, and during the week they sometimes have evening events. Also, you must be there two weeks before school starts to prepare for the next Rush. I'm taking 17 credits so I can graduate in four years, and I didn't know how I'd have time for classes, homework, other things I'm interested in, and the sorority.

I decided to stay Independent mainly because there were only a few sororities I really was interested in joining, where I felt I would fit in well, and I didn't get invitations to join those. I didn't want to just join others that invited me, because I thought I would regret it if it was not my ideal place. It's a pretty cutthroat process. I knew a lot of people who did not get asked back to more than one or two houses.

I was never dead set on being in a sorority. Even though I didn't join, I had a great time and met such nice people. My best friend and I met during Rush. Neither of us joined. And none of the other friends I made during Rush joined. Like me, none were invited to join sororities they were interested in.

It's easy not to be Greek here [Berkeley is about 10 percent Greek]. There are always people around, campuswide activities, many organizations, and Greek parties are open, so if you want to go, you don't have to be a member.

If you are at all interested, do Rush because you find some of the stereotypes about drinking and not studying are really not true. It's nice to assess Greek life for yourself and meet nice people along the way. For the friends you meet, $30 isn't much.

Maria Henning, University of California, Berkeley

Going Greek and Loving It

I had no intention of ever going Greek. My parents were Greeks at their respective schools, but the Greek system was not a big part of their lives, so they never talked about it. My conception of the Greek community came from *Animal House*, and that wasn't exactly what I was looking for. Freshman year, I moved into the oldest dorm on campus, an all-guys dorm. When you fill out a residential packet, you put your top five choices, and Bowles Hall was the last place I wanted to live. I was almost in tears when I found out that's where I was going to live. I had older friends who said the greatest part of their college experience was living in a coed dorm and meeting lots of different people.

But Bowles Hall ended up being the best experience ever. There were about 200 guys, and almost no one wanted to be there. The first day, you start bonding with each other and it became like a 200-person fraternity. We had exchanges with the all-girls dorm and other events, so there wasn't like a lack of girls, but I was finding that living in an all-guys environment is more laid-back. So sophomore year, I moved into a house with four other guys from Bowles, but something was missing. Some kind of spark wasn't there, even though we would go out. I had thought freshman year was so great that the next year could only get better, so this was a big letdown. I needed something to bring me back to the Bowles feeling. Fortunately, Bowles was a big recruiting center for fraternities, and a bunch of my friends had already pledged Kappa Delta Rho. So I went through Rush and automatically came here; I knew this was where I belonged as soon as I stepped foot onto the porch.

Bowles was filled with tradition, and so is KDR. That's really what binds members together and builds brotherhood. I go to alumni banquets with 80- and 90-year-old men; we have the same secret password, the same handshake. We do things the same way they did. We live by the same values of honor and integrity.

About 10 percent of the student population here belongs to the Greek community, but we provide a large percent of activities. Social outlets, philanthropy events, parties. If you want to meet people, this is the place to do it. I've been president of my house and vice president of the fraternities; going Greek empowers you to get involved on campus.

Todd Schwartz, University of California, Berkeley

End-of-Chapter Questions

19.1 What does "going Greek" mean?

19.2 What's the difference between a fraternity and sorority?

19.3 What are the advantages of joining the Greek system? The disadvantages?

19.4 What are the advantages of staying Independent? The disadvantages?

19.5 How can I get information about fraternities and sororities?

19.6 What are Rush parties? When is Rush?

19.7 How do I get invited to join the house I like best? What if I don't get that invitation?

20

Back to Being a
Freshman Again

You just spent 13 years studying your way from kindergarten through twelfth grade. Everybody's proud of you, and the family has suggested you take the summer off as a reward, right? Probably not. Most likely, you'll have a couple of jobs. One with an employer who will actually pay you; the other at home, sorting, remembering, pitching, shopping, packing, and saying good-bye as you prepare for one of the biggest transitions of your life: going to college.

There will be times when the summer seems endless. You'll be bored, anxious to move on, tired of the tedious routines and the expectations of home and family. There will also be times when the summer seems to disappear in a heartbeat. You'll feel devastated at the thought of leaving the familiarity of your life and petrified to face a future where nothing is even remotely familiar. The only thing certain is that late summer will show up and college will start.

What to Take—or Not
Take—to College

Chances are you walked through residence hall rooms during your campus tours, so you have a sense of size. Some schools provide incoming freshmen with a description of the living areas, including room dimensions, wall color, furnishings, and floor plans, or pictures on the Web site, probably under "Residence Life." You've probably also spoken with your roommate about who's bringing which big items. Taking all that into account, the words "scale down" should come to mind as you think about what goes to school and what stays at home. Unnecessary items in a small dorm room can lead to serious clutter and even create roommate conflicts.

Begin by deciding what *doesn't* go: clothes for every season (almost no students stay away for a year), that overstuffed chair you've curled up in for years (recheck room dimensions), and enough toiletries to last

Packing Tips

- ❏ All summer long, keep a running checklist of what you'll need, rather than trying to remember everything on packing day.
- ❏ If possible, find an unused but handily accessible place in the house where you can begin gathering items before it's time to pack.
- ❏ Come packing day—or days—consider which items in the to-pack pile are need-to-have and which are want-to-have. Advice: put the want-to-have things back in your room.
- ❏ Include a few special items from home, such as photographs.
- ❏ Use the backpacker approach when packing pants, skirts, and sport shirts. Lay the clothing facedown, fold back the sleeves, and roll up from the bottom to prevent creases.
- ❏ If you're taking any delicate items such as a party dress, lay each item facedown and place tissue paper on top. Fold the item with the tissue paper inside; add more layers of paper until the item is folded and completely wrapped in the paper.
- ❏ Duffel bags are easier to store at college than suitcases.
- ❏ If traveling by plane, because of random screening procedures, use plastic cable ties instead of locking checked bags; avoid overpacking, since the screener may have difficulty closing your luggage after inspection; spread out books and other documents in your baggage instead of stacking them; carry film onboard because some new screening equipment can damage undeveloped film.
- ❏ Check with the airlines for number of bags allowed and weight limitations.

until graduation day (your college is not in the middle of a storeless desert). Most colleges prohibit certain items for safety reasons: electrical cooking devices, halogen lamps, extension cords, and candles, including decorative candles. Wake Forest University in Winston-Salem, North Carolina, supplies each room with a combination microwave/refrigerator/freezer, called a "microfridge," so students can cook and store food safely.

If you think packing clothes for camp was tough, wait until you pack for college. You may receive a list from your school, and you will receive advice from your family. There are even Web sites with suggestions about what to take. Hobson's College View (www.collegeview.com/college/col legelife/campus/packing_list.html) seems to consider everything—clothing, organization and storage, personal documents, and so on. The study aids list includes a computer and printer, but check first regarding the situation at your college.

Besides clothing and the obvious necessities, schools suggest you pack UL power strips with circuit breakers, a shower bucket to carry toiletries to and from the bathroom, bed and bath linens, a desk lamp, hair dryer, memo board, clothes hangers, laundry bag, and lots of laundry detergent.

Finally, make and clearly mark a survival kit, just in case you don't get everything unpacked as soon as you land in the dorm. Contents should include toiletries, bedding, towels, and a couple changes of clothes. Oh, and maybe a set of basic tools and hardware. We remember one young woman who received a small tool kit as a high school graduation present. She thought it was the dumbest gift ever, but still packed it when she headed off for Tufts University in Medford, Massachusetts. Later, she said she met more people because they wanted to borrow her tool kit than she met at orientation.

Saying Good-bye

It doesn't matter how many people you say good-bye to, it's still tough. Some students say good-bye to their best friend, others to the 25 friends they can't live without; some say good-bye to a favorite uncle, others to the whole clan; some say good-bye to the teacher-turned-friend, others to three teachers, two coaches, the supervisor at work, and the next door neighbor for the last 15 years. It also doesn't matter how far away you're going—to the state college 30 miles north or a campus 2,000 miles east. You are leaving, and things will never be quite the same again.

A Father and Daughter Say Good-bye

It starts in May with the endless graduation parties. Then it's a summer of late nights, jobs, dates, and roving groups of hungry teenagers invading the house at all hours.

August it starts all over again with good-bye parties, late nights, and people coming and going at all hours. I'm going crazy.

Sometime in August everyone begins thinking about "the trip." How are we going to move all that stuff? What goes on and what goes in the car? Will it all fit? "Dad questions" mostly.

A summer of confusion is probably a good thing. There's not much time to dwell on the obvious. My daughter is leaving home. She'll be back many times, but it will never be the way it was. And it all happened too quickly. There was so much more we needed to talk about. All of this hits as you reach Pennsylvania. It's too late and you start to panic.

And then you're at college and your child changes right before your eyes. She becomes a capable and sensible young woman with a can-do attitude. Her room, a big city campus, her roommate, strangers everywhere, the endless admin lines—nothing seems to faze her. In fact, she's reveling in the experience! Maybe she was ready for this.

It's then you realize that she'll be just fine. It was all part of the plan when we started her life. Work with her, be there for her, teach her to be independent, able to stand on her own two feet. And that's what you tell yourself on the long, quiet ride home—she'll be just fine.

Eric Fogg, Clive, Iowa

After high school, saying good-bye to my parents, especially my father, was a difficult task. My dad, a strong, sensitive, and witty man, has always been one of my best friends. I am, in every sense of the word, a "daddy's girl." We share a very similar sense of humor, a love for good naps, and the same wavy hair. Leaving one of my biggest cheerleaders seemed like a frightening change for me. However, there comes a time when you have no choice but to go it alone.

The actual separation from my parents wasn't the waterworks show that I had expected. My parents left discreetly, and I can't even remember any sage advice they gave me. Instead, I began my college career with excitement and a little nervousness.

The difficult part began when I wanted to nail something into the wall and I couldn't find my hammer. And when the dining hall served a weak and disgusting replication of my dad's delicious pancakes. Those were the times that I knew I missed my dad and I wished he lived just down the hall again.

As I slowly figured out how to fix anything with duct tape, I called my dad to tell him my newest skill. My dad has become my best friend in a new way. He cheers me on in my endeavors halfway across the country. He checks up on my activities via phone and e-mail. I know for certain that when I do visit home, I can always find great dinner conversations, something to laugh about, and of course, the world's greatest pancakes.

Karen Fogg, George Washington University, Washington, D.C.

A Mother and Son Say Good-bye

At the beginning of the summer I was mad at him because he didn't get a job; he was just wasting his time. But he was being a high school senior and trying to do everything his way, kind of asserting himself, and that was so unlike him. He was getting us ready for him to leave home.

All during the summer we were busy getting ready to go for orientation in mid-September. But he pulled a fast one on us because he didn't want to be the last one of his friends to leave. He e-mailed Lawrence's soccer coach on his own and then told us he was going to try out for the team and needed to leave at the beginning of August.

Just John and I drove to Lawrence because when John decided to go early, his dad couldn't get off work. It was nice because I had eight hours driving with John. He told me he was serious about the girlfriend he'd been dating, which was a surprise to me.

We started moving in about 8:30 in the morning and were done by about 2:00. I got to make his bed, take his towels out, and put his socks away. Everything else he wanted to keep intact in their boxes and do it his way. He made that very clear to me. We've always been very close and he'd readied himself much more than I had.

I was dragging my feet and knew he was ready for me to say good-bye. Finally, it was a quick, teary good-bye and I walked alone down the stairs. When I got in the car, I called his dad and said it was the saddest thing I've ever done. I've experienced my mother's death and a miscarriage, but this was the saddest. But John wasn't sad.

I cried halfway home, and if it hadn't started pouring, I would have cried all the way home, but I had to concentrate on driving. I just had no idea how he was going to make out. But he didn't look back. I've always thought it was because of the school he picked. It was the right place, small, with a caring faculty—all the planets were aligned.

You can see growth and maturity every time we see him. When he comes home, he seeks me out, just to talk about his feelings and plans. That's extremely nice. So we're closer now than we were. But saying good-bye never gets easier and I always have tears.

Cheryl Giudicessi, Urbandale, Iowa

It was more or less overcast, in the mid-80s, the day my mom said good-bye and left my dorm room. I walked her to the stairwell. I was sure she was close to, if not in, tears; I was ready to move out and move on. It was probably harder on her than me. She went downstairs and I went back to my room and tried to get it organized. I expected it to be kind of depressing but just thought, "Look, I'm on my own and there's all this stuff I can do." And a half hour later I had a team meeting.

I had a unique situation because I played varsity soccer and moved in one and a half months early, in August, when only about 300 kids were on campus. We're on the term system so school doesn't start until mid-September, so I was without a roommate for about a month. I liked adjusting without a roommate.

I was just so busy that I was never homesick. A lot of it is going to a small school. It's like a family—you walk across campus and know everybody. It's not like walking out in the world or a large university and you know just 10 people out of thousands. I knew most of the kids here by the third month.

My orientation was mainly through the team. The upperclassmen show you the ropes, and the coaches make sure they do. When all the freshmen showed up in September, I went to the real orientation activities. There were exercises and icebreakers, such as going to a football game together and wearing the same shirt. There were also residence hall things to get to know people.

I missed my mom's cooking, nothing particular, just anything that's not dorm food. I missed coming home on weekends, talking to my parents before going to bed. My mom and eight of my high school buddies' moms pool stuff and send gigantic care packages to each of us three or four times a year. Anything can be in them—clothes, Best Buy certificates, disposable cameras.

When you say good-bye, try to not linger. Get the good-bye part over instead of dragging it out. When moving in and out, I tried to do it fast. I didn't let Mom organize my room—I did it the first night so I had something to do. Try to find something to occupy yourself for the first couple days, whether it's working out, playing a sport, whatever. I never had time to feel lonesome.

John Giudicessi, Lawrence University, Appleton, Wisconsin

Who's Homesick Now?

Unless you've spent extended time away from home before college, you're likely to be just a wee bit homesick. Almost everybody is, but they have different ways of showing or ignoring it. (Your parents also miss

Seven Ways to Beat the Homesick Blues

1. Finding your social niche in college can be tough. Whether your peers admit it, they are almost certainly struggling with homesickness too. That "I've got lots of new friends here" or "I'm perfectly together" attitude is probably a facade. Realizing this will not make you less homesick, but there is truth in that old adage about misery loving company.

2. Use free minutes on your cell phone to talk regularly—but not daily—with family and special friends. Knowing on a blue Wednesday that you'll be catching up on everything back home come Saturday can help. The first Sunday of Liz Schwab's college career, she called her parents in Fort Wayne, Indiana, at 8 p.m. Now long out of college and married, she and her parents still keep their Sunday evening commitment.

3. Get busy beyond the classroom. Join a club or group that shares your interests or background. Finding like-minded people will help you focus on something beyond being lonely.

4. Join a study group. Ask a few people in one of your classes if they'd like to form a group, or at least get together to prepare for that first test.

5. Missing good friends can be a big part of homesickness. Realize you probably won't have new best friends anytime soon—certainly not by the end of your first week on campus. Good friendships evolve from time spent together, experiences shared, and similar interests discovered. That's what you're looking for, and so is everyone else. Good friends will happen.

6. Perhaps you were a big fish in a little pond in high school. Now you may be a little fish in a big pond, which is a definite change. Instead of thinking about how unimportant you may feel, concentrate on the new opportunities before you. Dwelling on the positive can make days less difficult.

7. Consider your new life: You're in charge of your academics, all the commitments beyond classes, the laundry, checkbook, meals . . . it's likely that you've just taken on more responsibilities than you've ever experienced before. Figure out your priorities and how to achieve them. Managing time well boosts confidence and helps you begin to realize you'll be okay on your own.

Homesickness Happens

I am really outgoing and like to meet new people. I was always superinvolved in activities, so I always had someone to say "Hi" to wherever I went. I was expecting college to be this great experience where I would meet new friends and have fun being independent. But when I first got here, I was completely overwhelmed.

Orientation seemed pointless because I was meeting so many people I knew I'd never see again. It was so weird to walk down the street and not know anyone. In your hall you can say "Hi" but they don't really know you. You don't have anyone to explain what you're feeling or to have inside jokes with. It shocked me because it wasn't the fun time I'd imagined.

I missed the weirdest things. Back home I had always brought my boom box into the bathroom so I could sing to my CDs in the shower. I couldn't do that in the dorm.

I knew homesickness happens, but you have to realize there is a complete adjustment period for a couple months. The first two weeks you're just trying to figure out what's going on. You realize you aren't the only one—everyone has to deal with being homesick. Then you start to get in the flow.

But don't try to join too many activities or make friends too quickly. Let it happen. You'll talk to someone and hang out, and then you'll hang out a bit more. It just takes time to find people you mesh with. I noticed people who made really fast friendships weren't such close friends at the end of the year.

Try to do something you find relaxing like journaling, listening to music, running or working out. I like to nap and just close my eyes and not think about anything. I'd call friends at home on my cell phone, somebody to talk to who you don't have to explain everything about your story because they understand. As long as you are nice to people, you will find your niche. Just give it time.

Martha Edwards, Marquette University, Milwaukee, Wisconsin

your gear left by the back door, going to your swim meets or orchestra concerts. Their house is a lot quieter now even if you didn't hang around much during the summer.) Your feelings are only harmful if you wallow in your homesickness. But you're not going to do that because there's just too much to do at college.

You Do Go Home Again

When author Thomas Wolfe said you can't go home again, he was referring to the fact that people change, including the people at home and you. After even one week in college, you'll be different simply because of your experiences. The first time you return home, high school will be back in session without you, family routines will have continued without you, friends may or may not be around, and there's a LOT of homework and reading you have to accomplish. Internalizing these realities before you get home may help you avoid—or at least better deal with—the changes.

Five Ways to Feel Welcomed Home Again

1. Be allowed to sleep in the first Saturday back.
2. Have your folks fix your favorite meal.
3. Spend time with a best friend from high school.
4. Go back to your old haunts.
5. Round up some friends and go out for pizza and a movie.

September or December Timing

When you go home to visit, obviously, depends upon distance and finances. Unless you're at a school where most students go home on the weekends, you'll be missing some of the flavor of college if you leave every Friday afternoon and return on Sunday evening. Plenty of freshmen return for high school homecoming or maybe Halloween; others wait until Thanksgiving or even Christmas. Most students probably travel back and forth more their first semester, or even their first year, than later. As the campus becomes your new home and your college classmates turn into friends, you'll make fewer trips back and forth.

"But I Don't Have a Curfew in College"

Shades of last summer, you're still being told when to come home! Here's a typical conversation between the parent and the college freshman.

PARENT: "You need to be home by 1 a.m."

STUDENT: "But I don't have a curfew in college. Heck, when I'm at school, you don't even know if I've gone out and you sure don't know what time I get back to the dorm."

PARENT: "True, but you're not at college now."

Most likely, the conversation occurs not because your parents don't trust you, but rather, because they worry about you. And if they're still alive when *you're* 70, they'll still be worried about you. Try for a mutual

---

Coming Home Again

I grew up in a suburb of Des Moines. I was involved with horses from a really young age, even though nobody in my family had previous horse experience. [Loving horses] was part of what influenced me to choose this school. I didn't even know about it until I was taking my ACTs and was asked where I wanted results sent. I wanted to come out West, so I marked a couple Montana schools, saw the University of Wyoming and added it. Then I researched it more. I wanted to venture out, do something I'd never done before.

It's 680 miles away from home, and if anything, the distance made coming here more exciting. I can't go home on weekends, which makes going home more special.

The first time I went home was two months after school started. During fall break. I was dating a guy, so we drove home and surprised my mom. It was a five-day break and we drove 9½ hours each way. It wasn't awkward coming home but I knew it would be different, but I didn't know how. My room wasn't really my room anymore, but Mom went out of her way to make sure she was at home for me and cooked what I liked. It was like having a birthday for three days in a row.

Coming home made me realize I'd really left the nest, and made me want to see my family. Moving so far away has brought me a lot closer to them. [I think] Mom noticed a change in my wanting to be at home. Like staying up until eleven o'clock talking to my parents.

If it is even a small thought in your head about going far away, you should pursue it. Don't do what your older siblings did or what your parents want you to do. You have to follow your heart.

Jenny Walters, University of Wyoming, Laramie

agreement about a curfew, or promise to call them if you're going to be very late. And come in quietly. They'll sleep better.

End-of-Chapter Questions

20.1 How will I know how much stuff my dorm room can accommodate?

20.2 Should I take clothes for every season? Shampoo for a year?

20.3 Where can I find a list suggesting what to bring to campus?

20.4 Why should I have a survival kit?

20.5 What's the best way to handle the big job of packing? What do I need to know if I'm traveling to college by plane?

20.6 How can I deal with homesickness?

20.7 Why will it be different when I go back home for a visit? How should I handle that curfew issue with my folks?

Index of Questions

Chapter 1: Who You Need to Know—and What You Need to Do

1.1 Besides parents, who can help me with my college search and applications? How much input should other people have in my decisions?

1.2 How can teachers help me? Do I have to earn an A in their class for them to want to help me?

1.3 Which people outside of school might help me? How?

1.4 Do I have to ask people to help or will they just do it? How well do they have to know me to help me?

1.5 If I'm friendly with a teacher, does that mean I'm brown-nosing? Will the teacher think I'm just sucking up to get a good recommendation or grade?

1.6 What factors should influence the classes I take?

1.7 What classes do colleges expect to find on my transcript? Are admissions requirements the same for every college?

1.8 Why should I consider taking some elective classes? Do colleges think you are goofing off if you take electives?

1.9 What is an AP class? An Honors class? What do such classes mean in terms of college preparation? How do colleges regard such classes for admission purposes?

1.10 How do I know if a college will give me class credit for my high school AP classes?

4.5 Have I checked costs for plane tickets and other travel? Does studying abroad sound exciting? How do I investigate costs?

4.6 Will my family's health insurance cover me at college? Do I need to purchase the college's health insurance plan?

4.7 What information do I need to perform online calculations for projected college costs?

4.8 What is the FAFSA? Is there a fee?

4.9 Is the FAFSA only for students below a certain income level?

4.10 When can I send in the FAFSA? Will I get a FAFSA decision faster online or by sending a paper application?

4.11 What's included in the Student Aid Report?

4.12 What if our Expected Family Contribution is too big?

4.13 Do colleges and the government expect me to pay for part of my tuition even if I qualify for financial aid?

4.14 Do I understand the parts of a financial aid package? Must I accept all parts of the financial aid package? Is it appropriate to negotiate with schools about financial aid packages?

4.15 Should I choose a college based on the best financial aid package?

Chapter 5: Scholarships and Managing Money

5.1 Who awards scholarships and grants?

5.2 How do I find out about scholarship opportunities? Which scholarships am I most likely to get?

5.3 Do I need to pay back scholarship and grant awards?

5.4 Should I sign up for a credit card? Do I have the necessary income to pay the bill each month? How can I compare credit card fees?

5.5 Do I know how to make a budget?

5.6 What are the advantages of having a credit card? What are the pitfalls of having a credit card?

5.7 What should I do if I can't pay my credit card bills?

Chapter 6: "I Am So Stressed Out!"

6.1 What exactly is stress, anyway?

6.2 What are some physical, emotional, and cognitive signs of stress?

6.3 What's an example of positive stress? Negative stress?

6.4 What are some of the causes of stress that I see in my own life?

6.5 What are some of the ways I can relieve stress?

6.6 When should I think about seeking outside help to handle the stress in my life? Where can I go for outside help?

Chapter 7: College Information—It's Everywhere!

7.1 What kinds of college search information can I get on the Internet? How can I sort out which Web sites will be helpful to me?

7.2 When I find similar schools, do I run side-by-side comparisons for a more thorough understanding of each school's qualities?

7.3 What personal information should I include in my basic profile? What personal likes and dislikes should I consider?

7.4 Do I have a major (or two) in mind? If yes, what are they? If no, what topics sound appealing as I look over the vast array of possible majors?

7.5 If no major sounds appealing right now, what other factors should I research in this beginning phase of the college search process?

7.6 How frequently should I touch base with my counselor so that he or she knows me by name and by need? Do I consider how busy my counselor may be with all those other students? Should I make appointments ahead of time?

7.7 How do I utilize all the information from my counselor?

7.8 How can I best use those big college books?

7.9 Can my parents come to the counseling office when they need information? How faithful are my parents and I about attending counselor sessions geared toward families?

7.10 When I learn about college fairs in my area, do I mark them down on the calendar? Should I attend them with or without my parents?

8.12 If I am considering a community college as a step toward transferring to a four-year school, have I checked the community college's accreditation? Will my class credits transfer to the four-year schools in which I'm interested? Is English 101 academically equal to English 101 at the four-year college I might transfer to?

8.13 Do I know if the community college has a steady number of students transferring to any particular four-year school?

Chapter 9: Parameters for Choosing Colleges

9.1 Why should I consider big schools and small ones at this point? What factors are important to me regarding size?

9.2 How many miles from home is the farthest college that I'm interested in? How many hours to drive? What does an airline ticket cost today?

9.3 What's my experience with being far away from home and family, whether for a short or long time? How many times would I want to come home before the winter holidays?

9.4 How do I function in familiar versus new and different surroundings?

9.5 How many courses specifically in my areas of interest are offered by the different size colleges I have looked at?

9.6 Do I have a major in mind? What draws me to that field? If I don't have a major in mind, am I being pressured to name one? Do I understand why people are pressuring me? Do they understand my point of view?

9.7 Is cost a factor at this point?

9.8 What would be the advantages and disadvantages of considering a faith-based school?

9.9 Have I spoken with anyone who attends a religiously affiliated school?

9.10 What would be the advantages and disadvantages of considering a single gender school? Have I spoken with anyone who attends a single gender school?

9.11 What is the difference between military academies and other colleges? Have I spoken with anyone who went through a military academy?

9.12 How ethnically diverse is the student body and faculty? How important is that to me?

9.13 Are there specific centers or organized groups for the various constituencies on campus—from Democrats and Republicans to gays and lesbians?

9.14 How do I differentiate hearsay from fact when it comes to a school's reputation?

9.15 What kinds of internships do students get in the areas that interest me?

9.16 What is the graduation rate in four years, five years, and six years?

Chapter 10: SAT, ACT, and Other Tests

10.1 What is the difference between the new SAT and the ACT?

10.2 What is the SAT II? Do I take the SAT II the same day as the new SAT?

10.3 How do I know which tests are required by colleges in which I am interested?

10.4 When should I take the tests? Can I retake the tests if I don't score well?

10.5 How should I prepare to take the tests? Are test prep classes recommended by my counselor?

10.6 Are test prep classes just for those aiming for highly selective colleges? If I'm not going to a highly selective school, how can a test prep class benefit me?

10.7 Where can I find online information about the ACT and SAT? The PSAT/NMSQT and PLAN tests?

10.8 When should I take the PSAT and/or PLAN tests? Will my counselor automatically tell me or should I ask?

10.9 Have I talked to my counselor about any of these standardized tests?

10.10 How do I register for the SAT and ACT?

10.11 How long do I have to wait before I can get my score? Can I get it online or only by mail?

Chapter 11: Campus Tours Make a Difference

11.1 Do I have access to college tour trips sponsored by businesses, my high school, or particular colleges?

11.2 What's my high school's policy on being absent to visit colleges? During my campus tour trips, how will I keep up with my homework?

11.3 Since our first contact, has the college admissions office consistently been helpful in planning my visit?

11.4 If I'm an athlete, have I arranged to meet with the appropriate coach? If I'm in an extracurricular activity (debate or drama, for example), do arrangements include the opportunity to meet with the appropriate faculty person?

11.5 If I have a particular interest (leadership opportunities or playing bassoon in the band, for example), do arrangements include the opportunity to meet with a student who is pursuing that interest on campus?

11.6 If I require special services (hearing or visually impaired, handicap accessibility, learning disabilities), do arrangements include the opportunity to inquire about these accommodations?

11.7 During the tour, did students, staff, and professors seem friendly, reserved, or not interested in each other?

11.8 What do the buildings look like—inside and out? Are freshmen guaranteed dorm space?

11.9 What about health center staffing, hours, services? Are visits covered by insurance?

11.10 Does the Greek system dominate the campus, share space with Independents, or is it even visible?

11.11 How's the dining hall food? Are there options for various dietary needs and preferences?

11.12 If my heart's set on a profession that requires a graduate degree (doctor, lawyer, research biologist, for example), how many of the college's students get into graduate programs, and where? (No, it's not too early to consider those scenarios!)

11.13 Is the community surrounding the campus appealing?

11.14 Whatever the campus atmosphere—liberal, conservative, serious, laid-back, straight, funky—did I feel comfortable?

11.15 Did it seem to be a party school? Are there Friday and/or Saturday classes?

11.16 Are the school and I a good match academically, so I'm neither bored nor chained to the library 24 hours a day?

11.17 Is it appropriate for me to call or e-mail the college admissions officer with any additional questions?

11.18 Can I discern important differences among the colleges I visited?

11.19 What three things do I like best about each school? Give an example for each.

11.20 What three things do I like least about each school? Give an example for each.

Chapter 12: The Campus Interview

12.1 How do I find out whether a school offers one-on-one interviews?

12.2 How far ahead do I need to make an appointment for the interview?

12.3 Do I know the date and time of my interview? Do I know how to get to the interview, including where to park? Where will my parents be during the interview?

12.4 Have I developed a vision of myself that I want to leave with the admissions officer? Do most of the points I want to make tie in with that vision?

12.5 Am I prepared to talk about what I've gained from my involvement in extracurricular activities or athletics? How can I put my best self forward without sounding cocky or like a braggart?

12.6 If I have experienced a particularly traumatic event, is there a counselor, teacher, parent, or other adult in my life who can help me decide whether or how to incorporate that into the interview?

12.7 How do I respond to open-ended or ambiguous questions such as, "What would you most like to accomplish?" and "What do you hope you're doing five years from now?"

14.3 What should I write about? How profound does the essay have to be?

14.4 Who should I ask for input on the essay topic and to critique my essay?

14.5 Can I work with my parents on this or will I be better off seeking help outside the family? Should I use an essay writing service?

14.6 How do I get over writer's block?

14.7 What approach works best for beginning my essay—an anecdote, an example, or a statement of fact or belief?

Chapter 15: Getting Accepted—or Not

15.1 How do colleges notify students about acceptance or denial? Have I discussed with my parents/guardians which of us has dibs on finding out first?

15.2 Do I understand the financial aid package offered by each school that has accepted me? Which school offers the most scholarship and grant funds that I do not need to repay? Which offers more loans and work study funds?

15.3 What are the pros and cons of each school, and how do they stack up against the aid offered?

15.4 How do I typically handle rejection? Do I blame others or let them help me climb back out of the pits?

15.5 If I get accepted and my best friend doesn't, what should I say? How can I be supportive?

15.6 What's a good backup plan if I don't get into my first-choice school? What makes my first-choice school so appealing? Why is it more appealing than other schools that have similar qualities?

15.7 Have I considered options in case I'm wait-listed or deferred?

15.8 Does putting off college for a while sound good to me? Why? What can I learn, where can I go, what can I do during a year off that will move me forward?

15.9 What's the best way to approach my parents about postponing college?

Index

About the Authors

Mary Kay Shanley has served on state and regional boards of education and spent 12 years as a school board member.

Julia Johnston is a journalist with over 20 years of experience writing for newspapers and magazines.